salamander
dream

by hope larson

Salamander Dream created by Hope Larson
Published by AdHouse Books.
Copyright © 2005, Hope Larson.

isbn 0-9721794-9-6
10 9 8 7 6 5 4 3 2 1

Design: Chris Pitzer
pitzer@adhousebooks.com

AdHouse Books
1224 Greycourt Ave.
Richmond, VA 23227-4042
www.adhousebooks.com

First Printing, August 2005.
Printed in Canada.

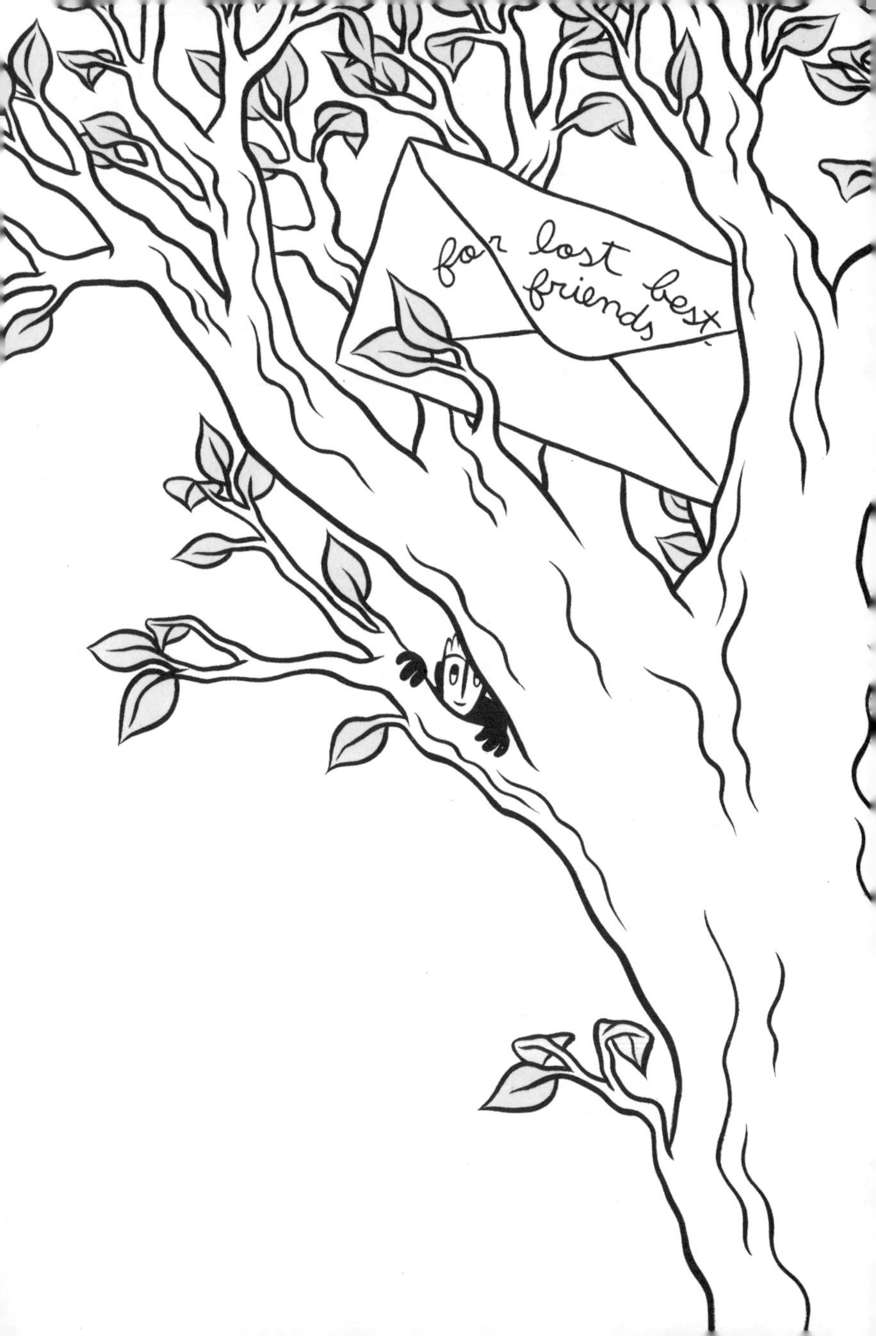
for lost best friends

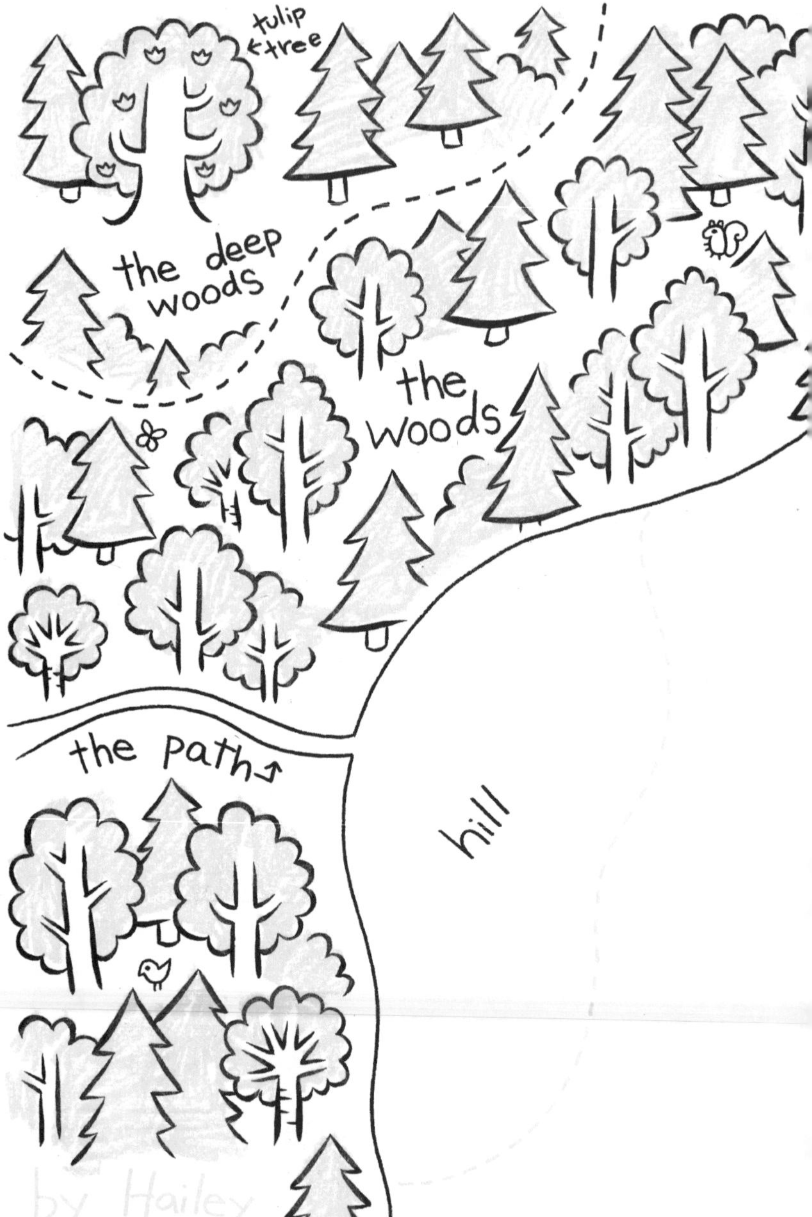
tulip
tree
the deep
woods
the
woods
the path
hill
by Hailey

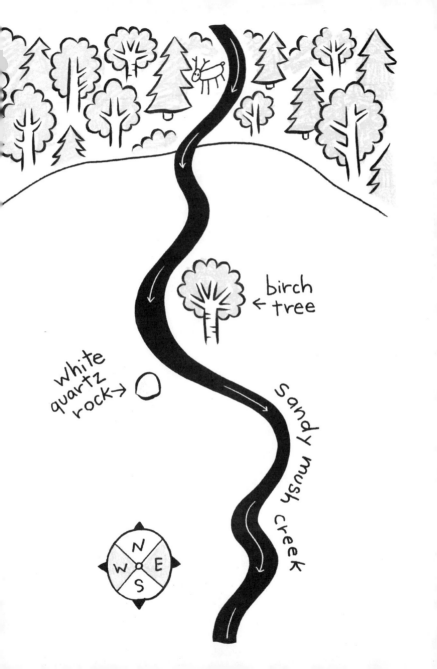

birch ← tree

white quartz rock →

sandy mush creek

N
W E
S

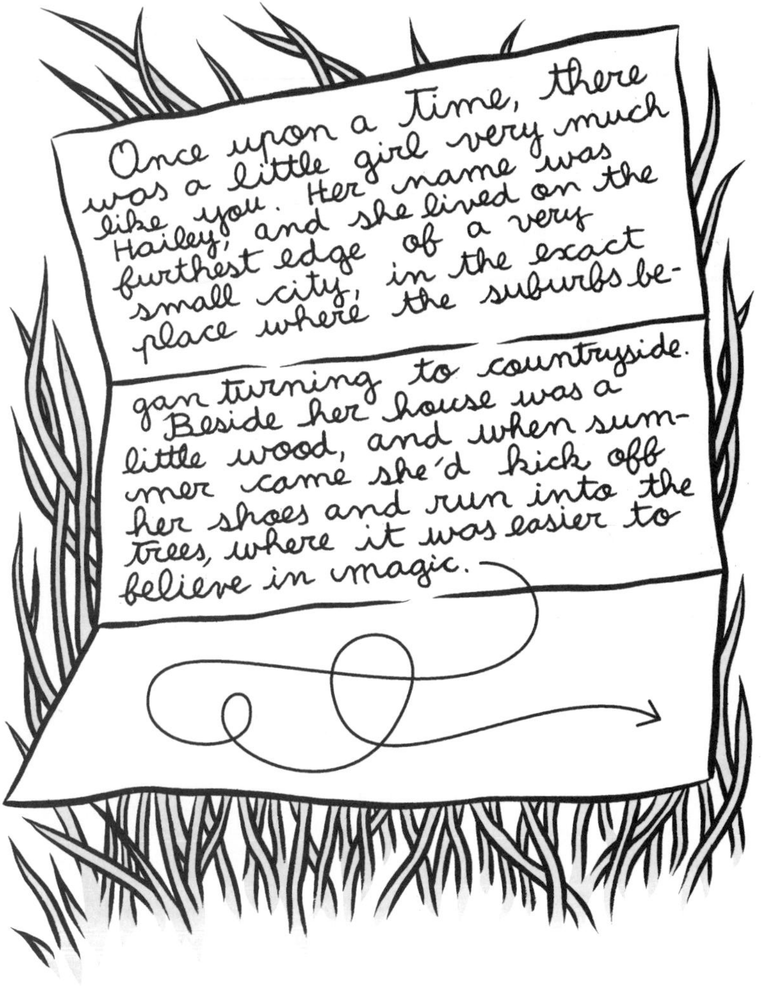
Once upon a time, there
was a little girl very much
like you. Her name was
Hailey, and she lived on the
furthest edge of a very
small city, in the exact
place where the suburbs began turning to countryside.
Beside her house was a
little wood, and when summer came she'd kick off
her shoes and run into the
trees, where it was easier to
believe in magic.

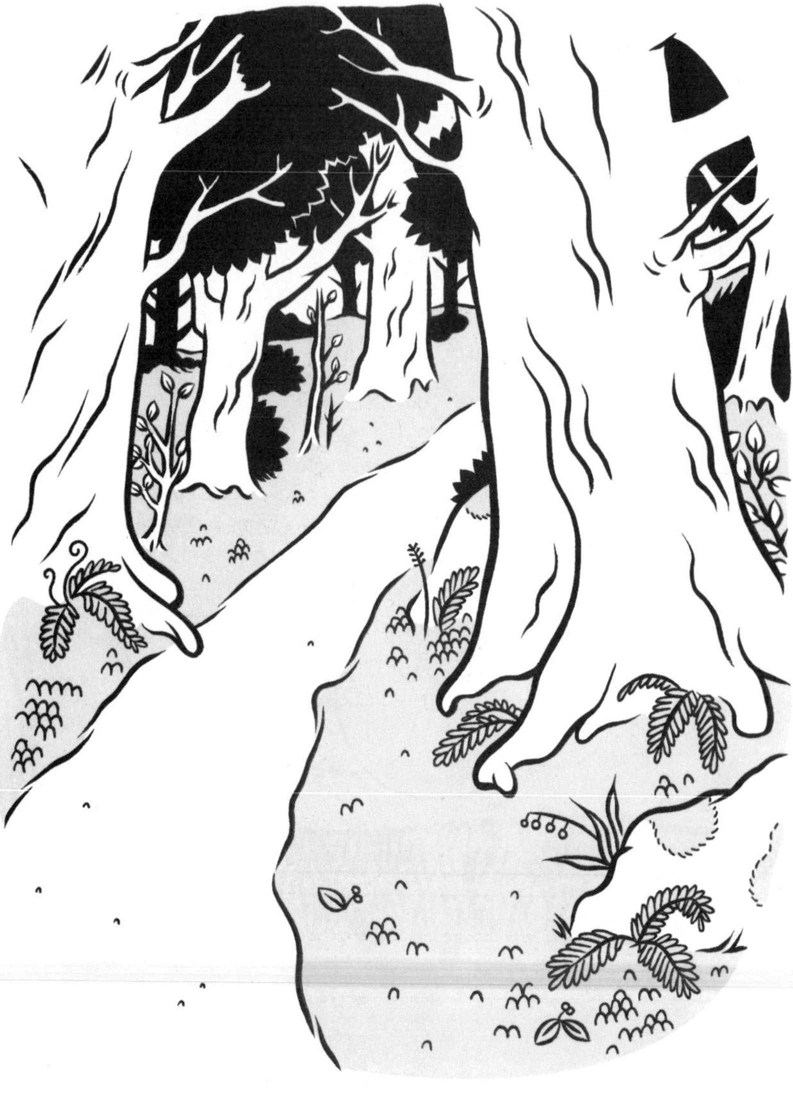

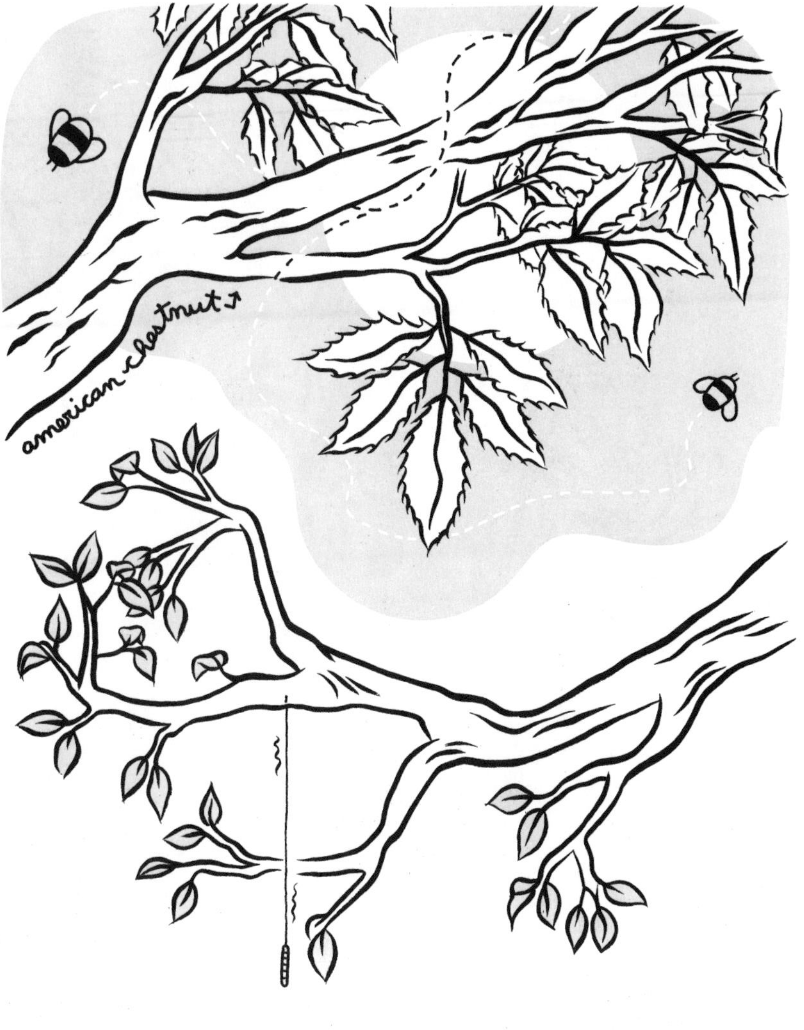
american chestnut ↗

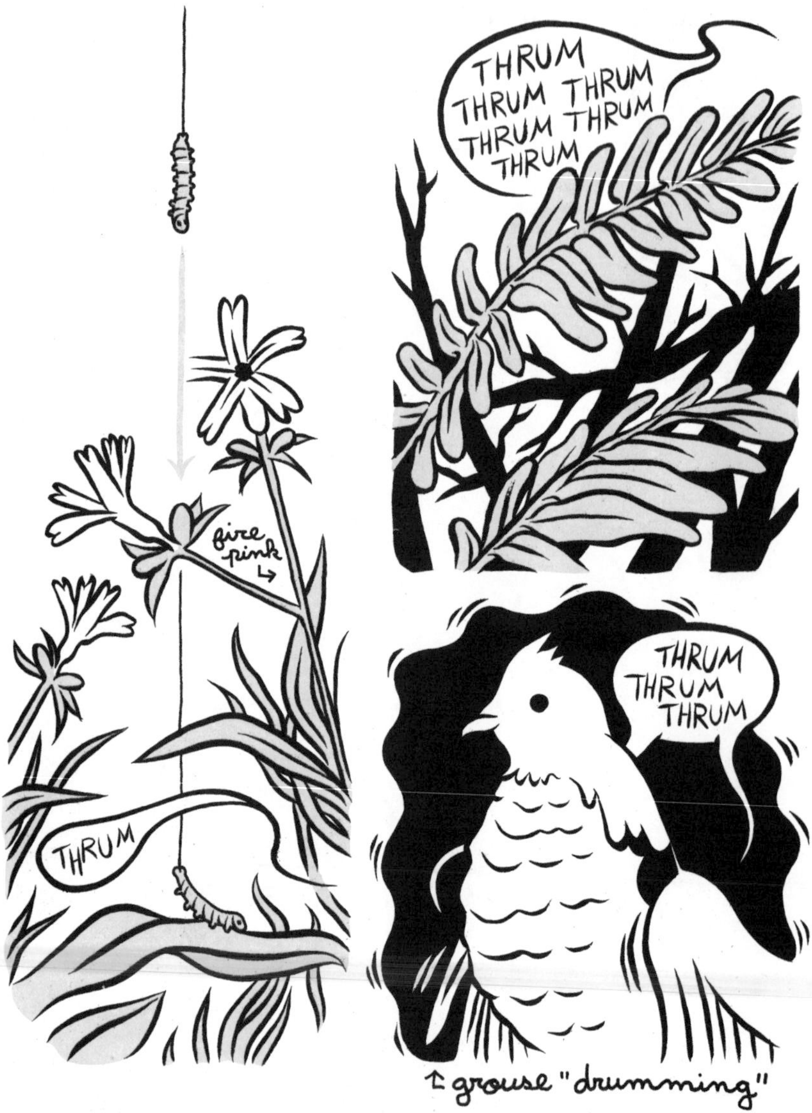
fire pink
THRUM
THRUM THRUM THRUM THRUM THRUM THRUM
THRUM THRUM THRUM
grouse "drumming"

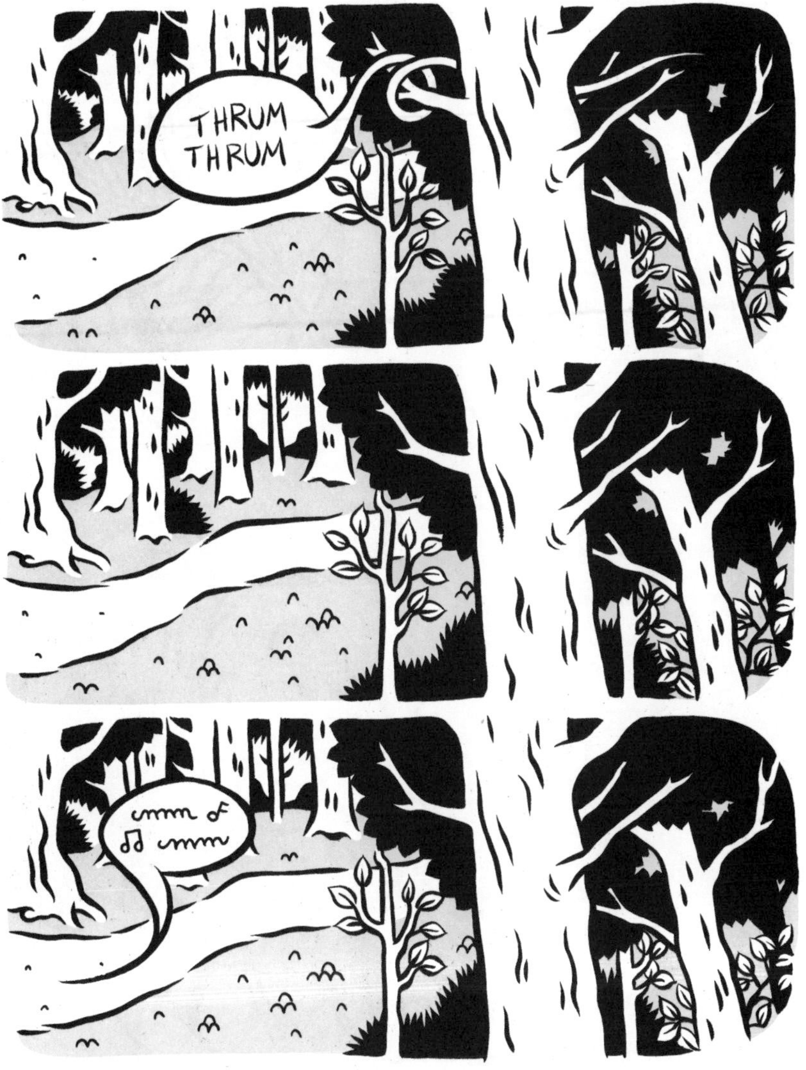
THRUM
THRUM

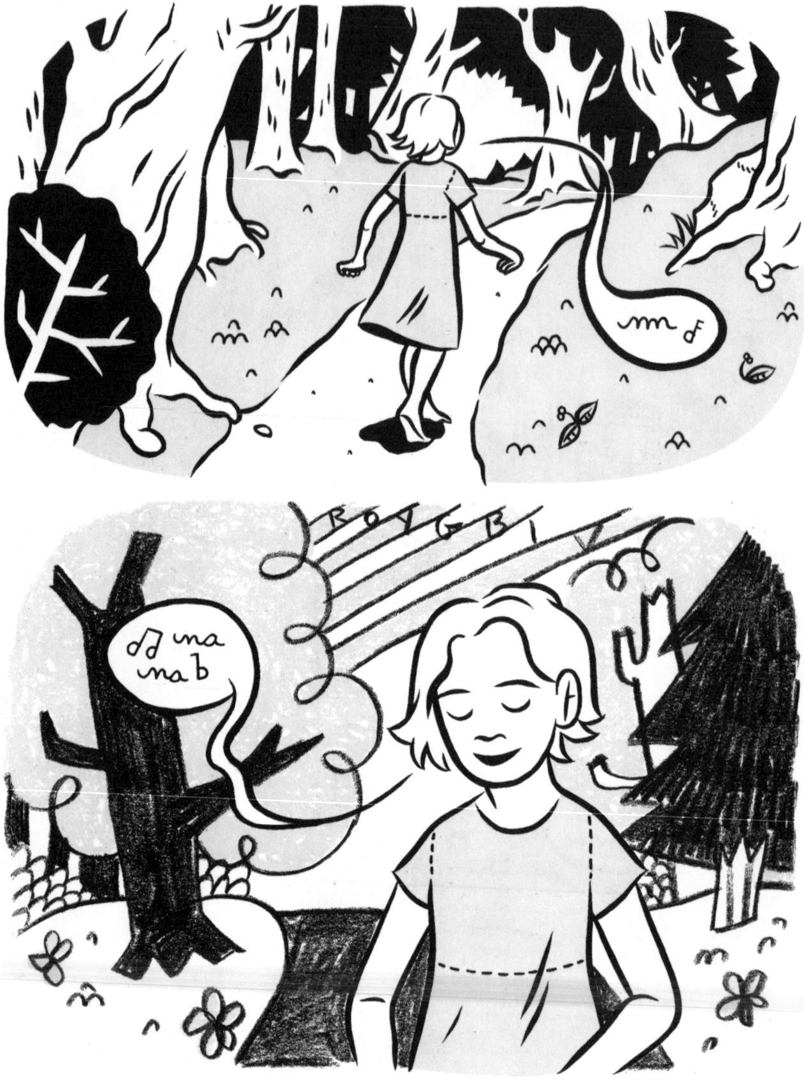
R O Y G B I V

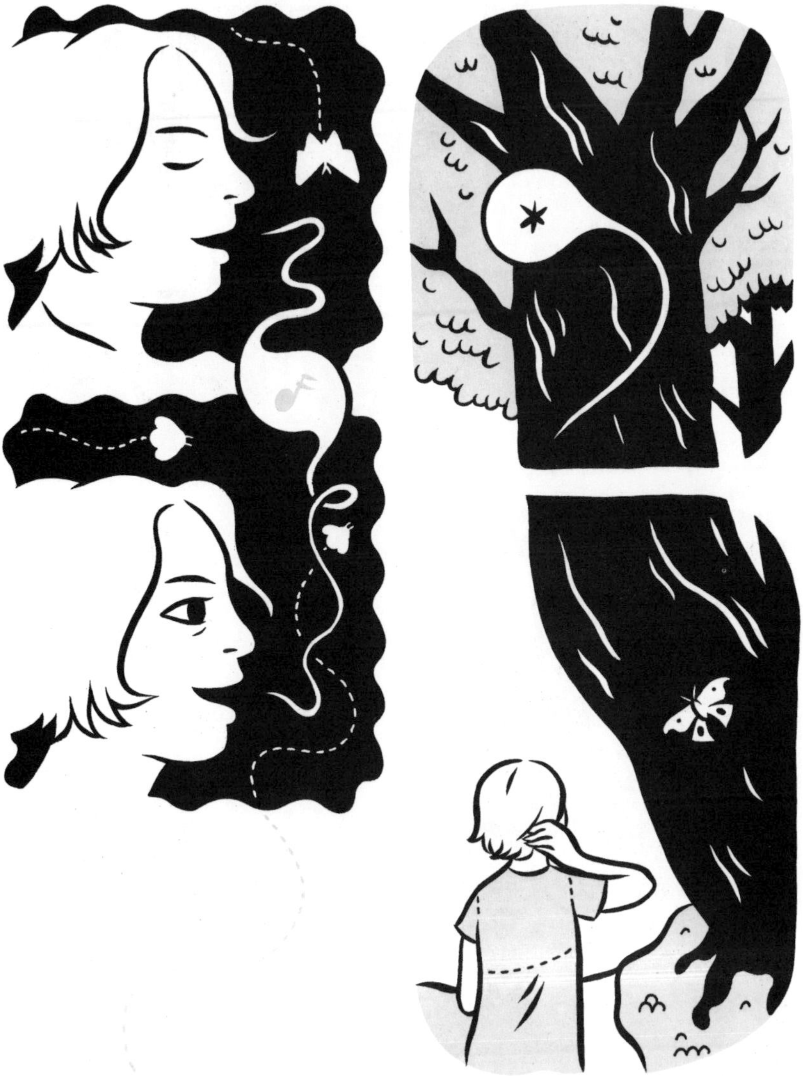

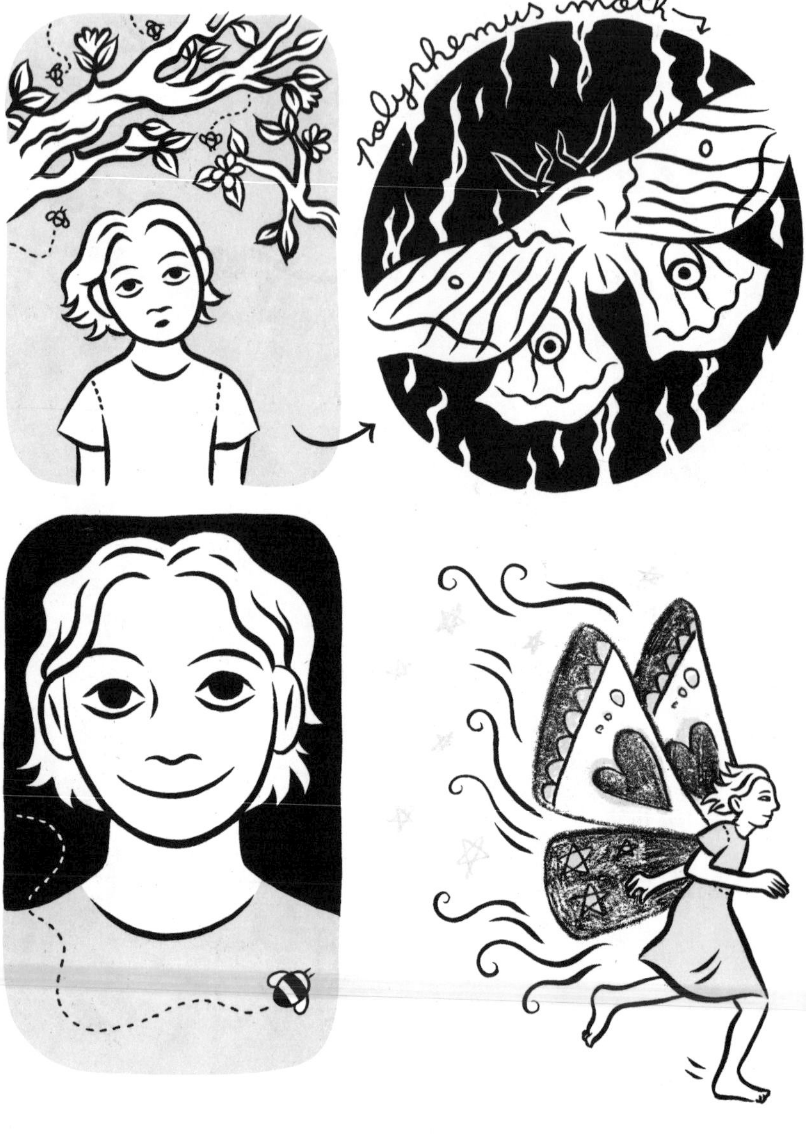
polyphemus moth

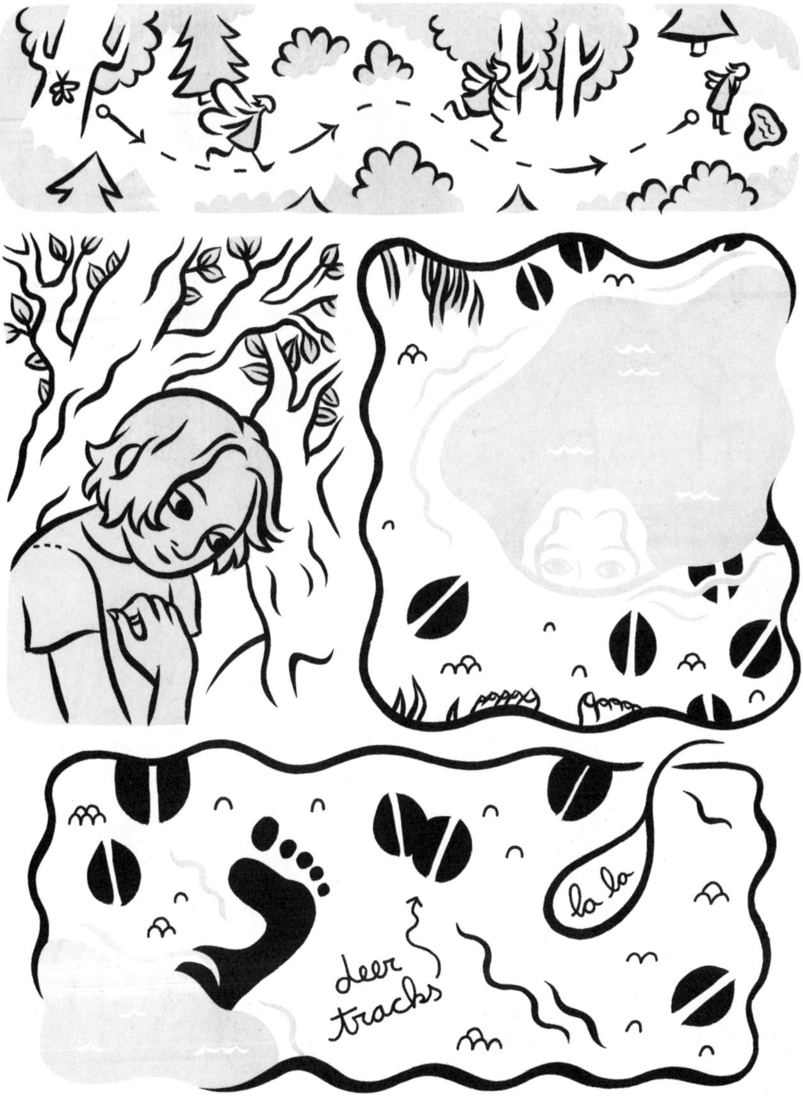
la la
deer tracks

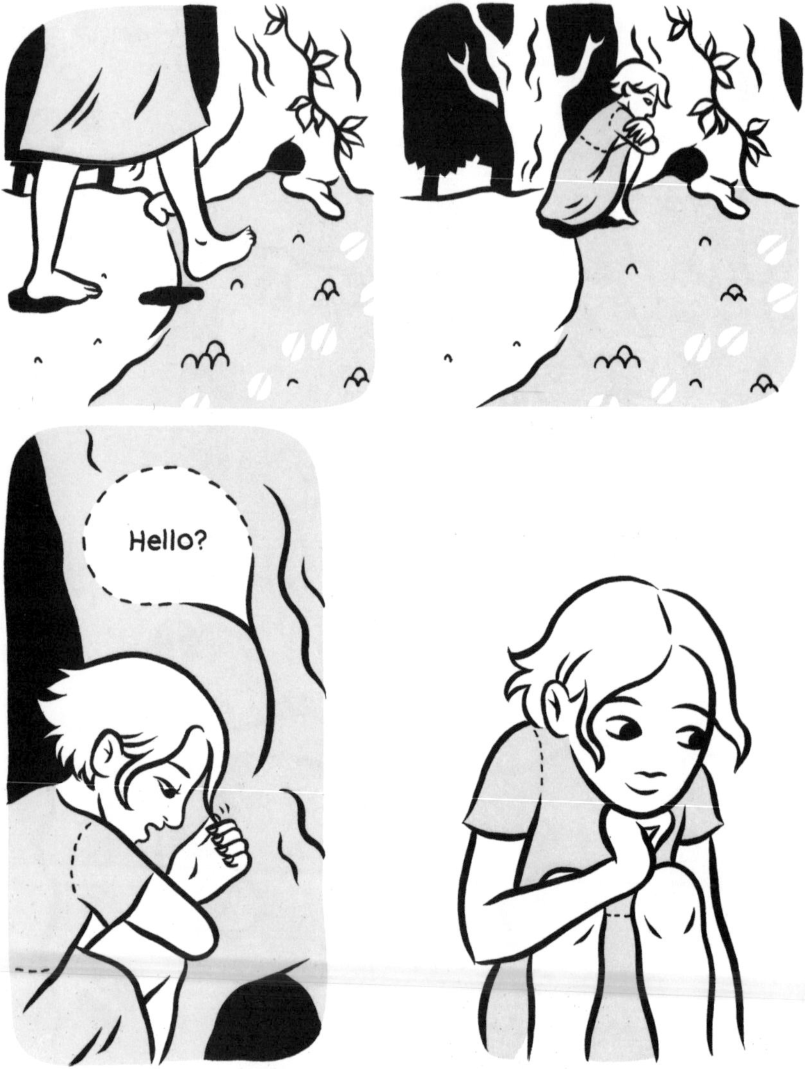
Hello?

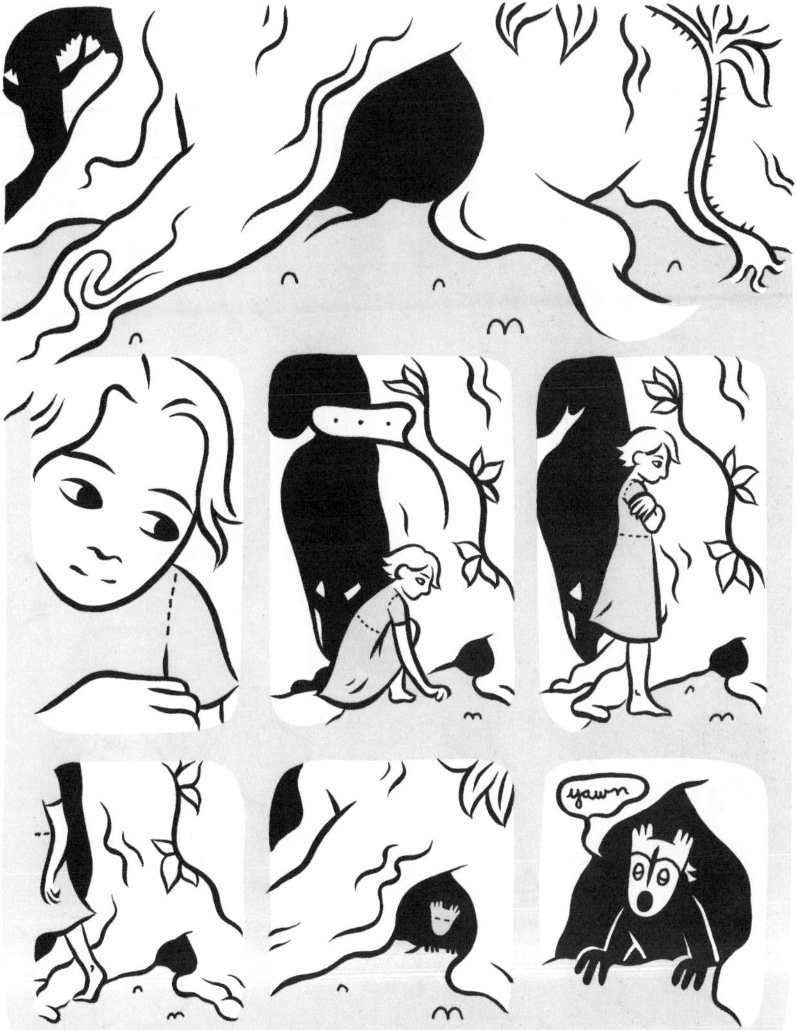
yawn

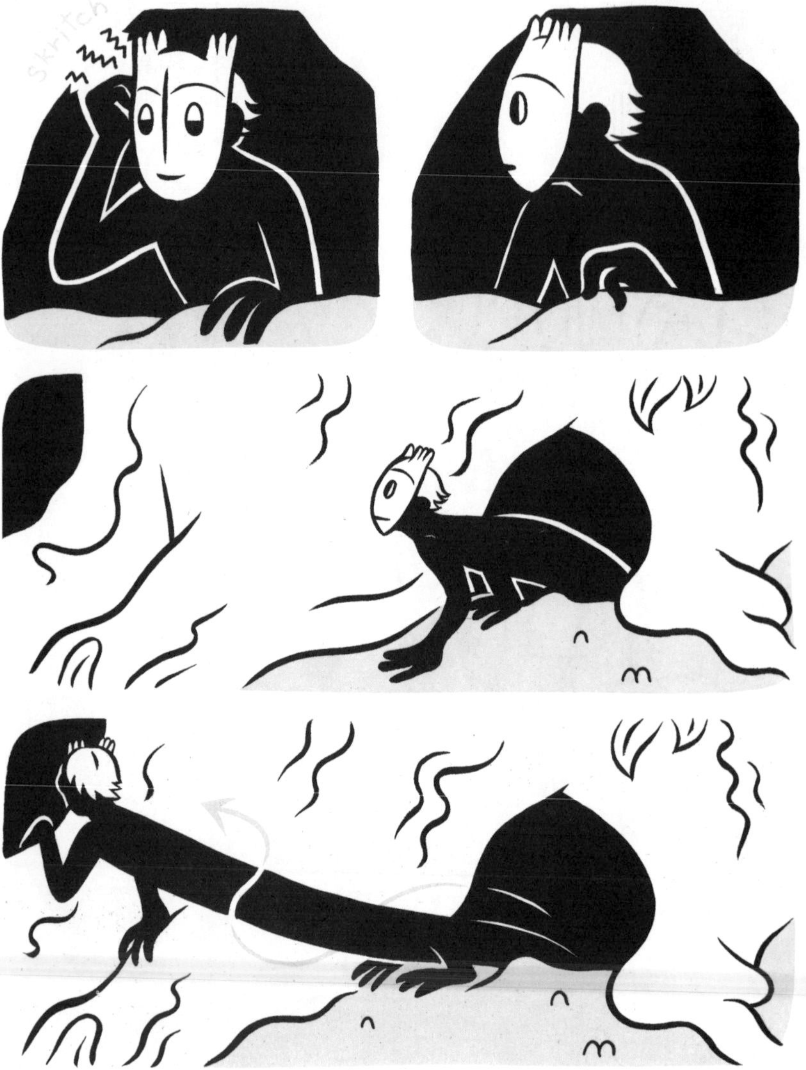
skritch

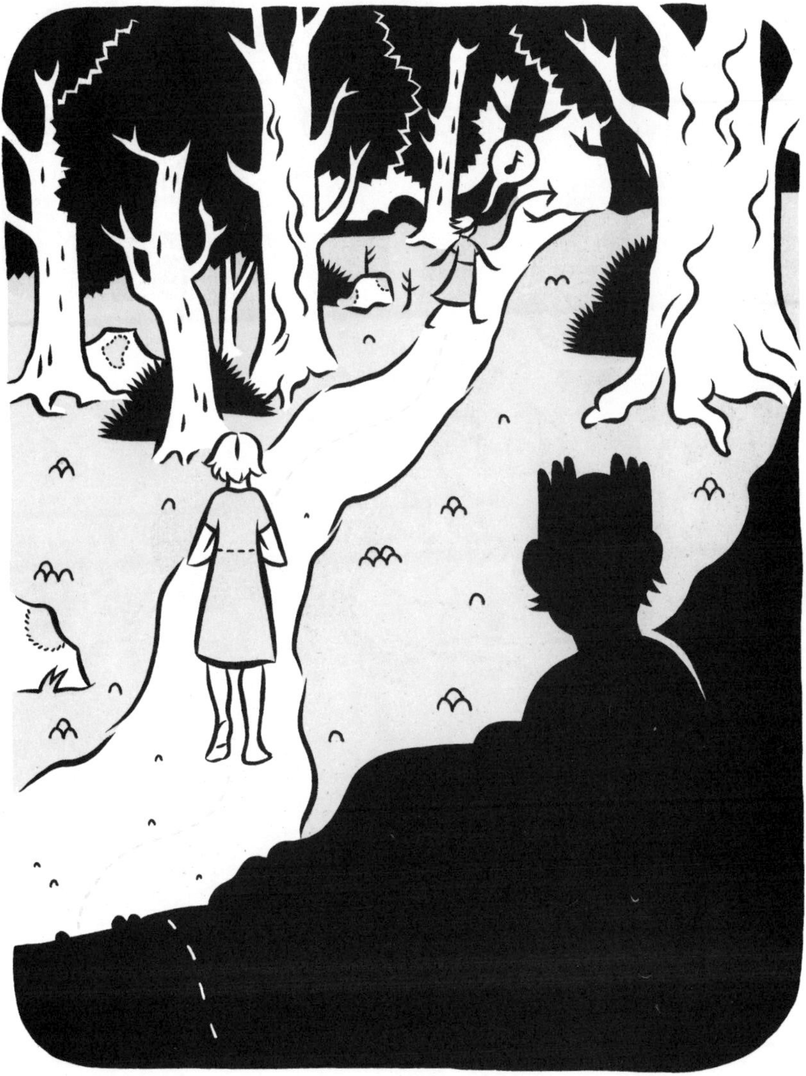

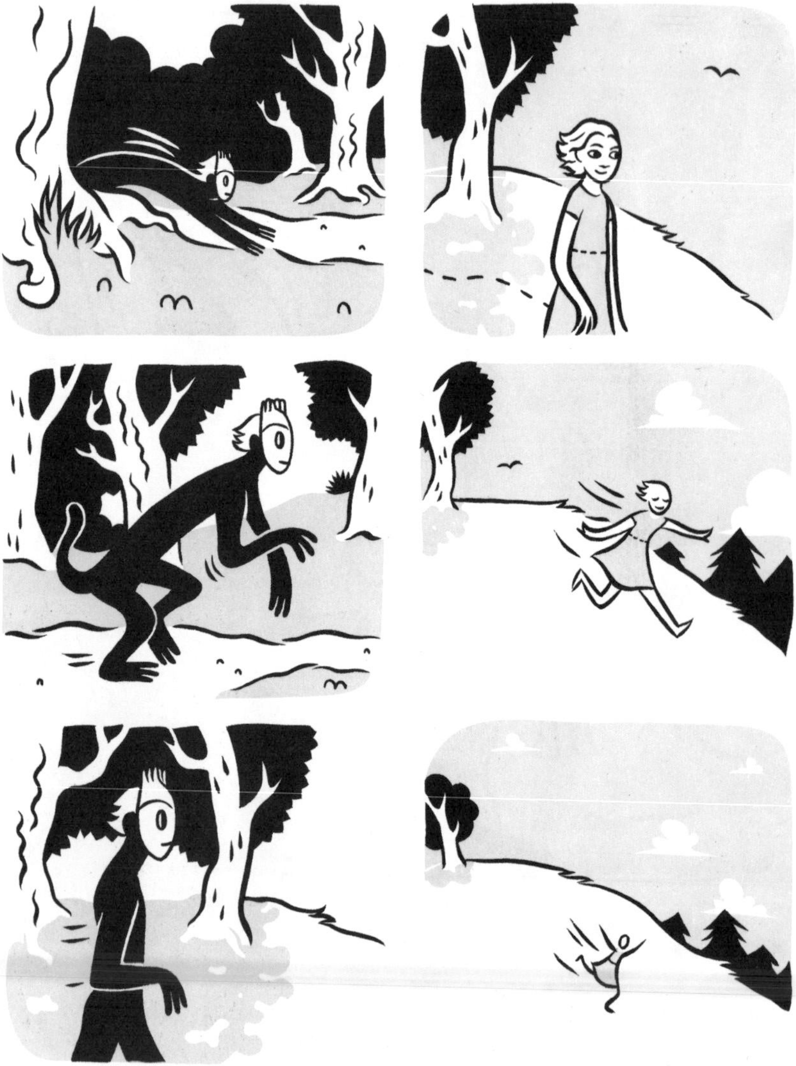

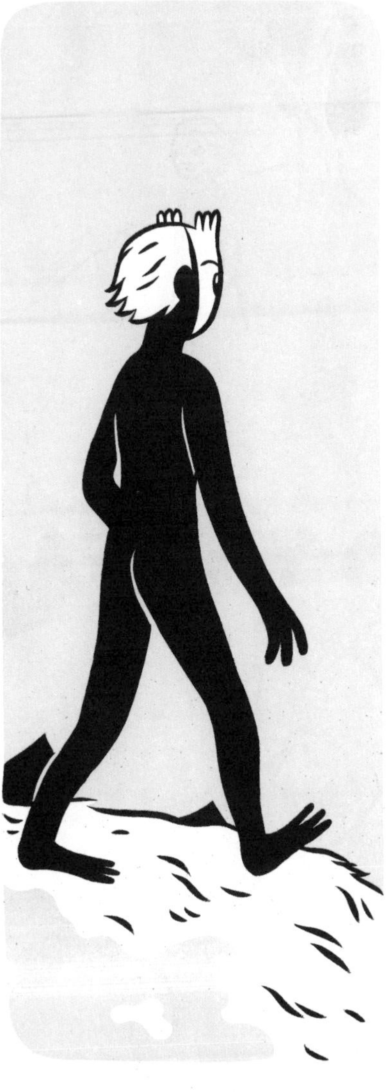

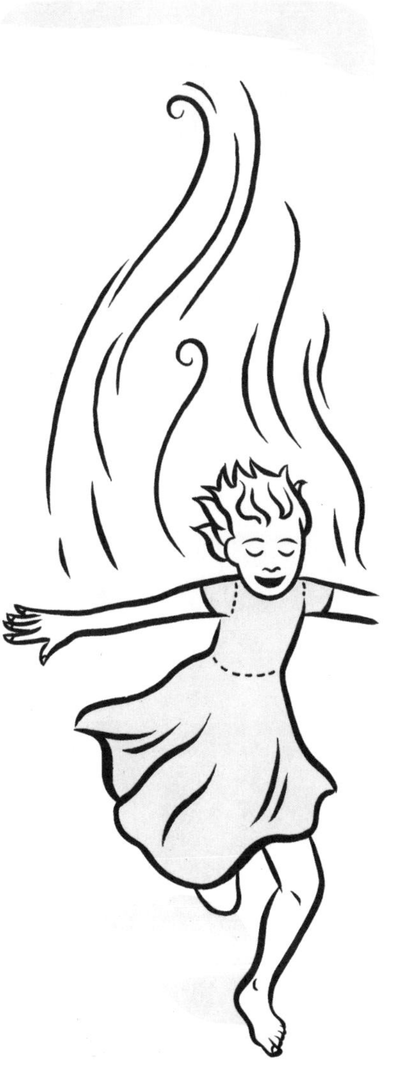

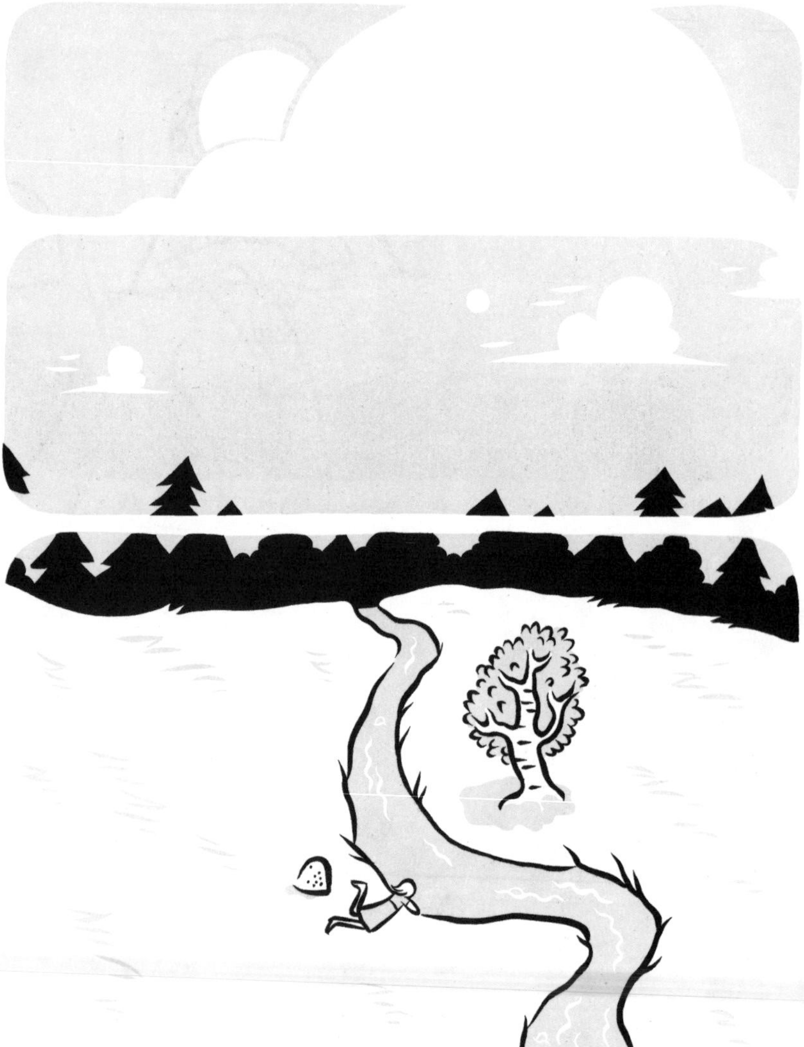

water strider

whirligig beetles

17

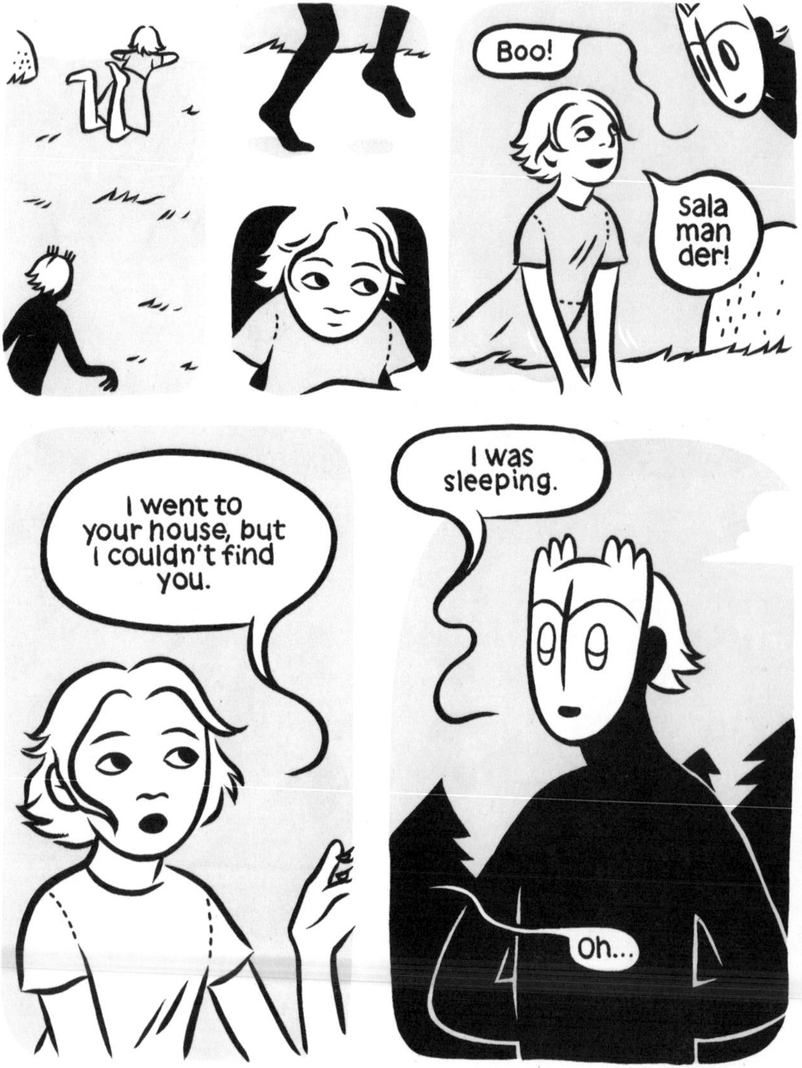
Boo!
Sala man der!
I went to your house, but I couldn't find you.
I was sleeping.
Oh...

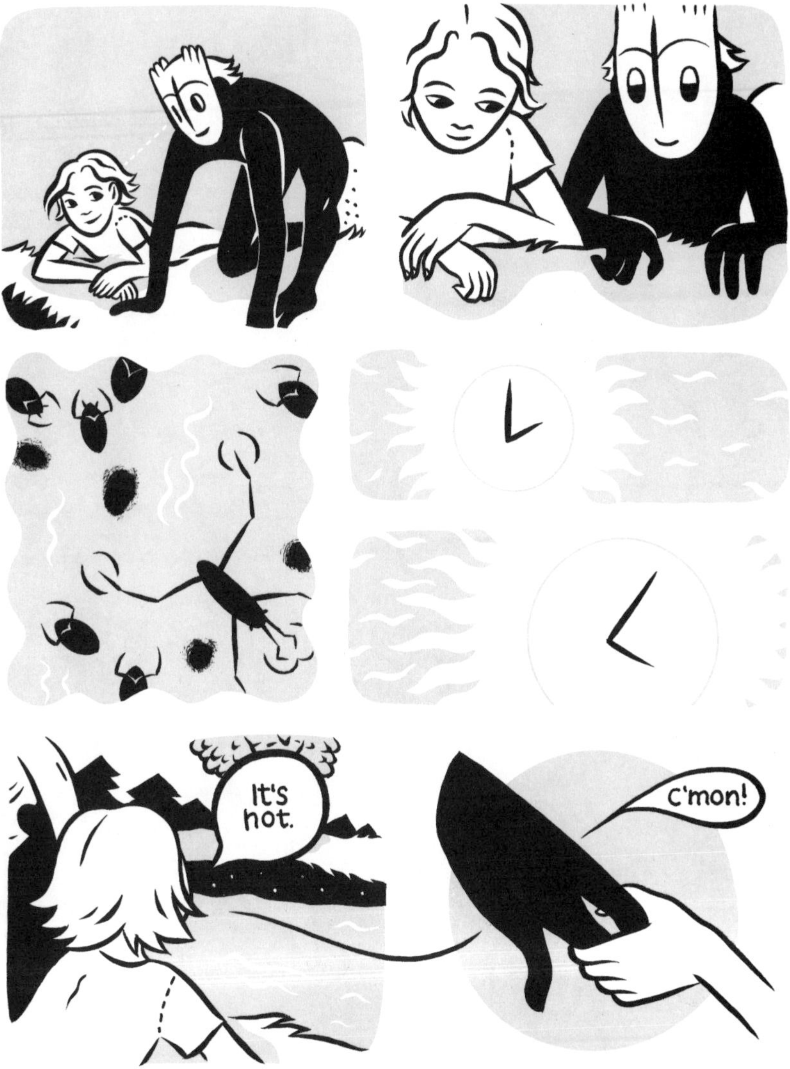
It's not.
C'mon!

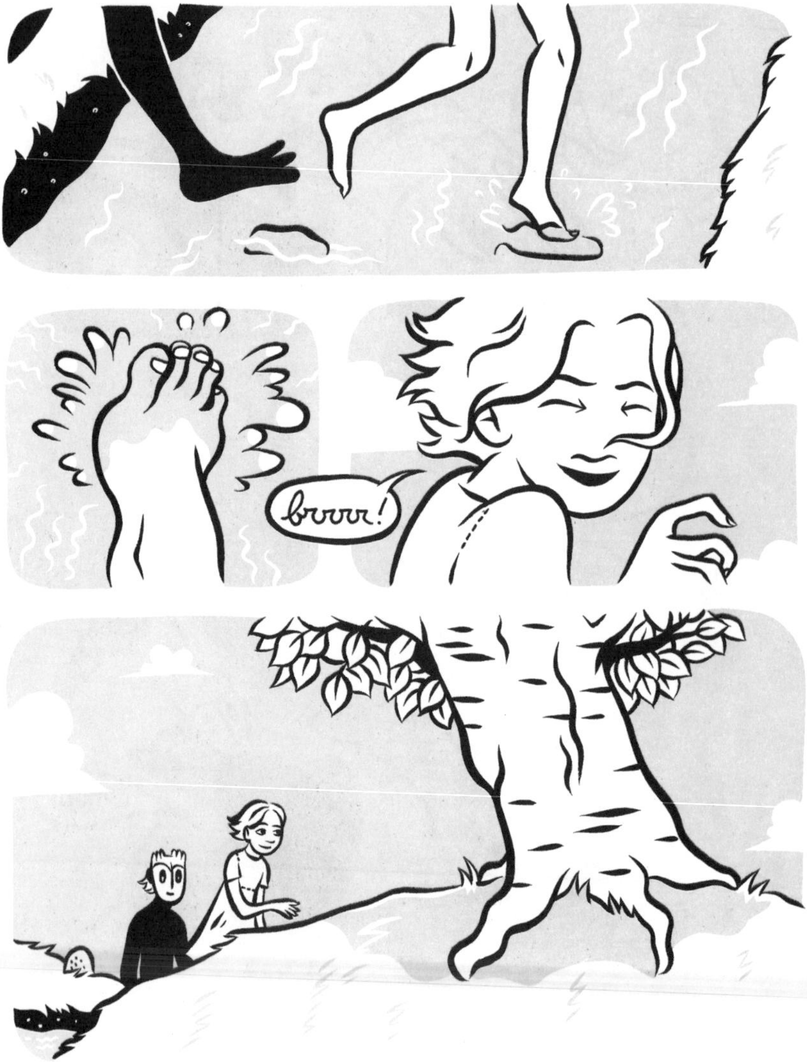
brrrr!

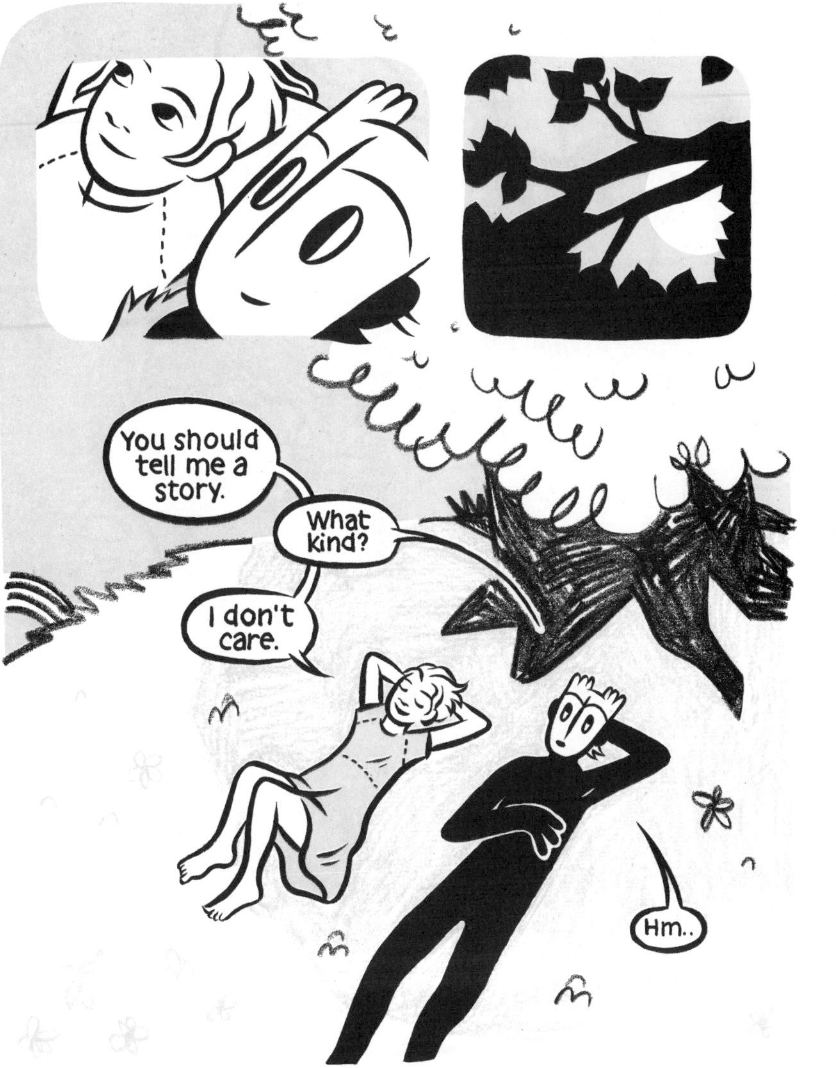
You should tell me a story.
What kind?
I don't care.
Hm..

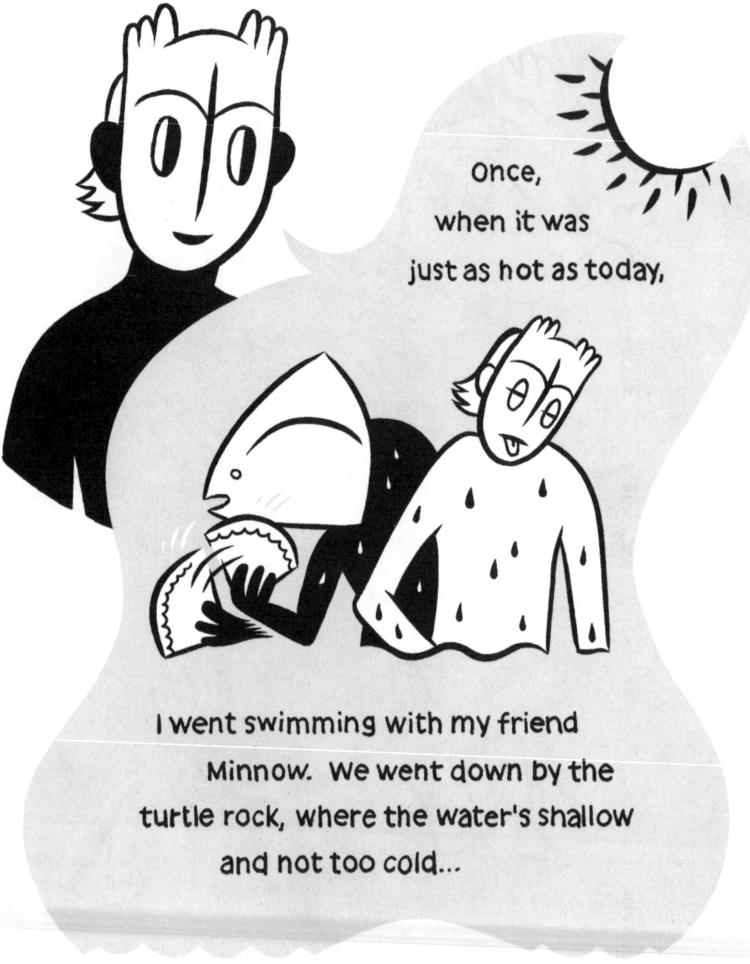
once,
when it was
just as hot as today,
I went swimming with my friend
Minnow. We went down by the
turtle rock, where the water's shallow
and not too cold...

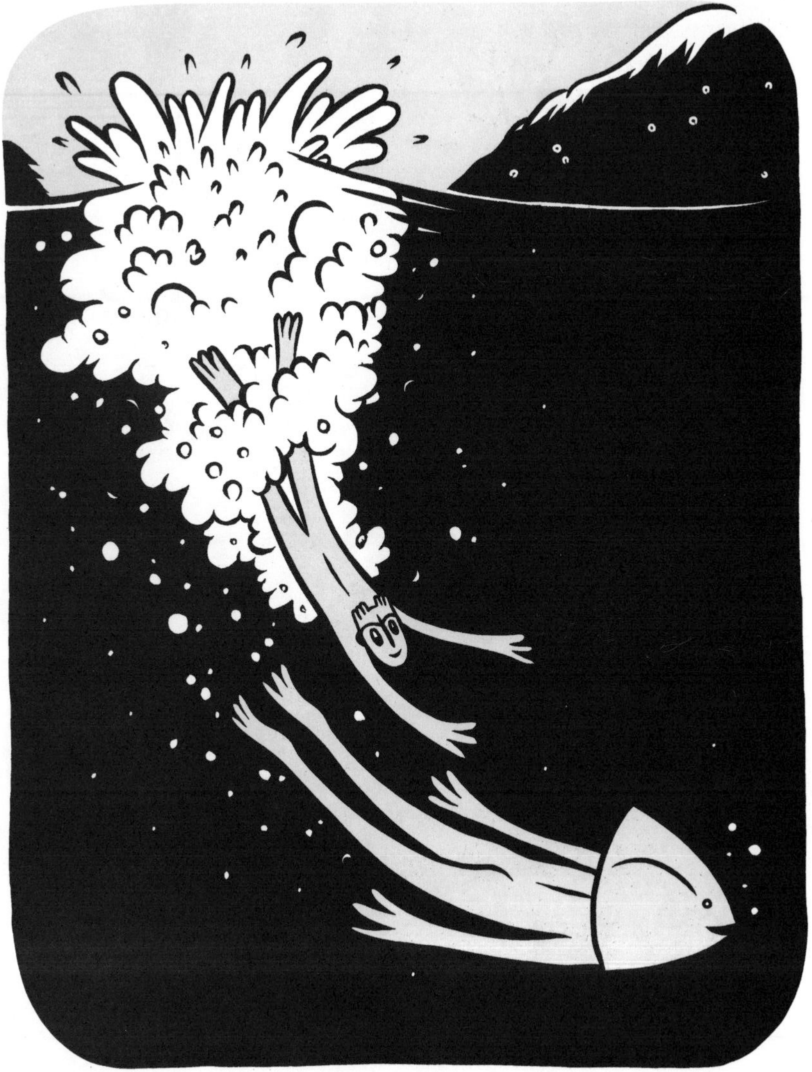

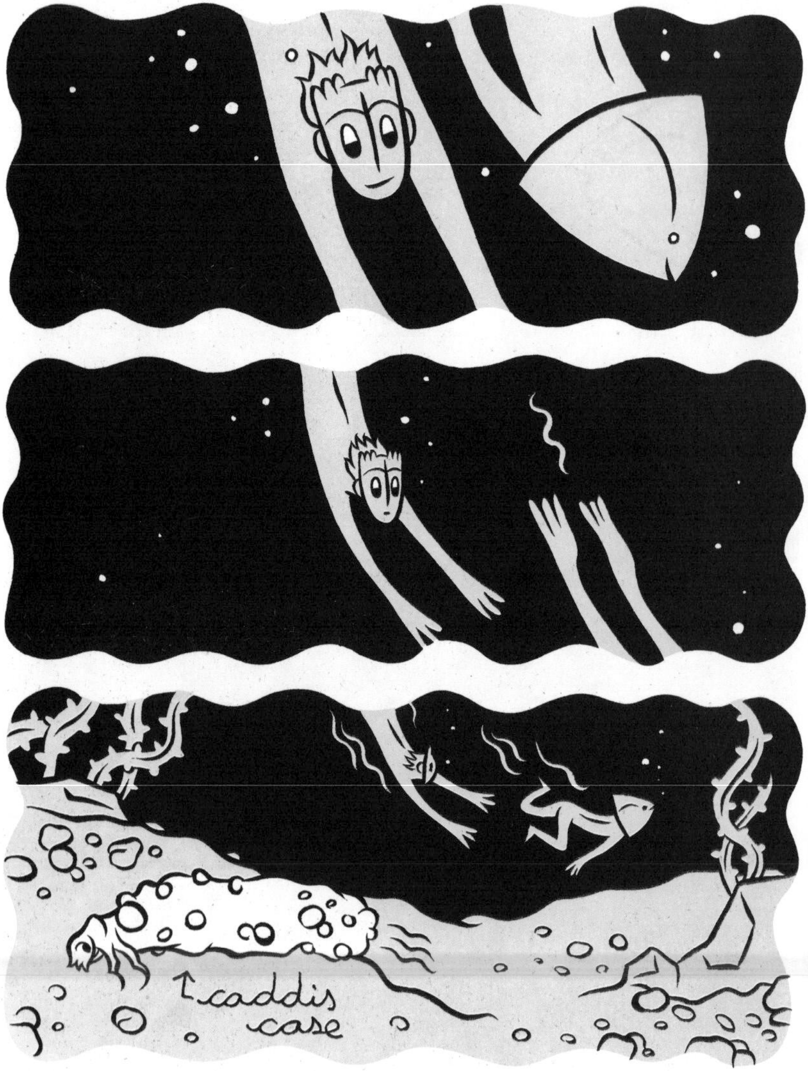
↑ caddis case

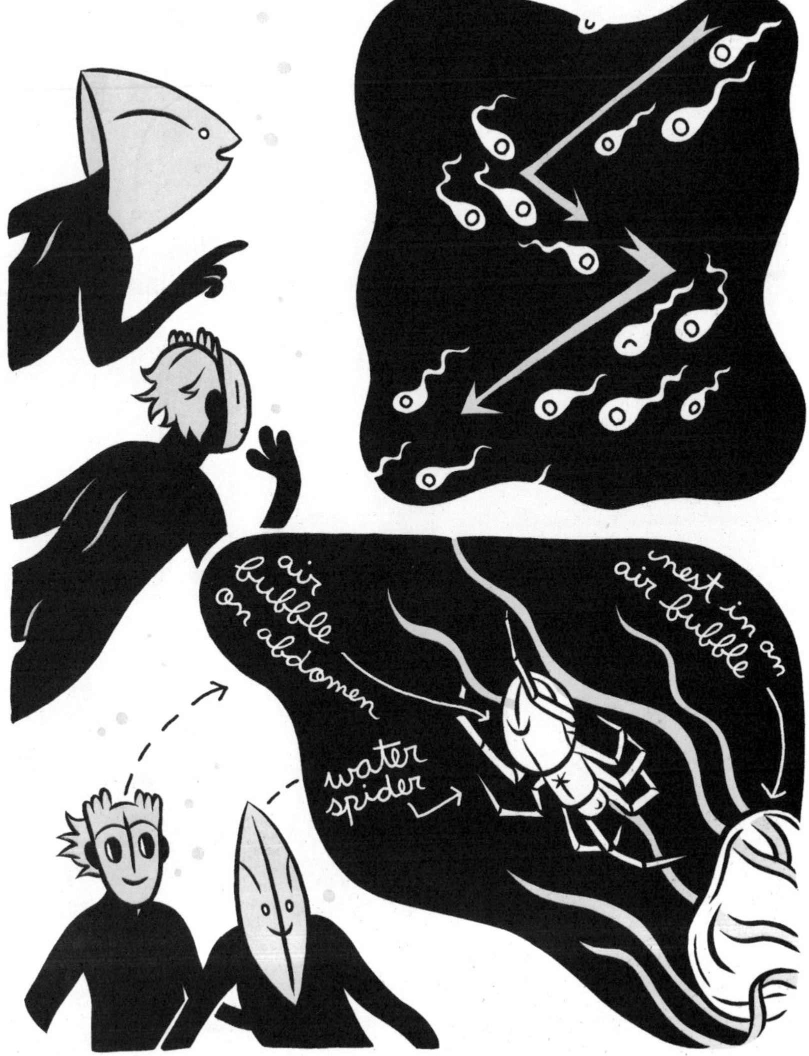
air bubble on abdomen
nest in an air bubble
water spider

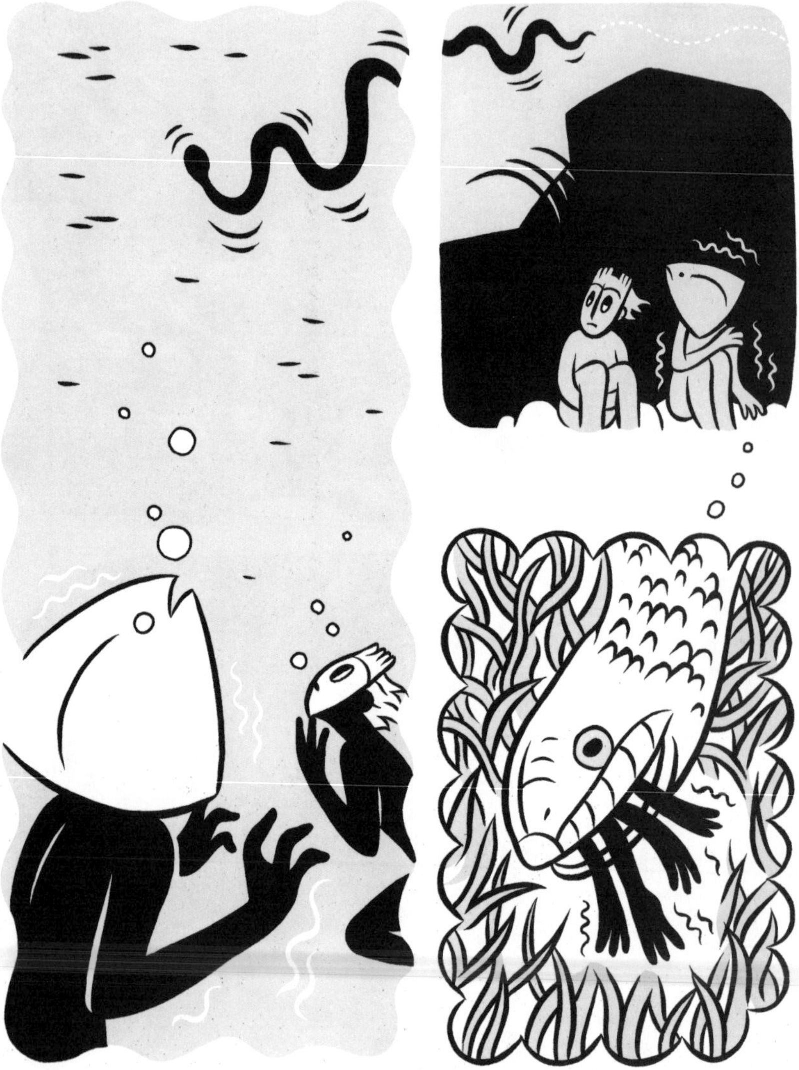

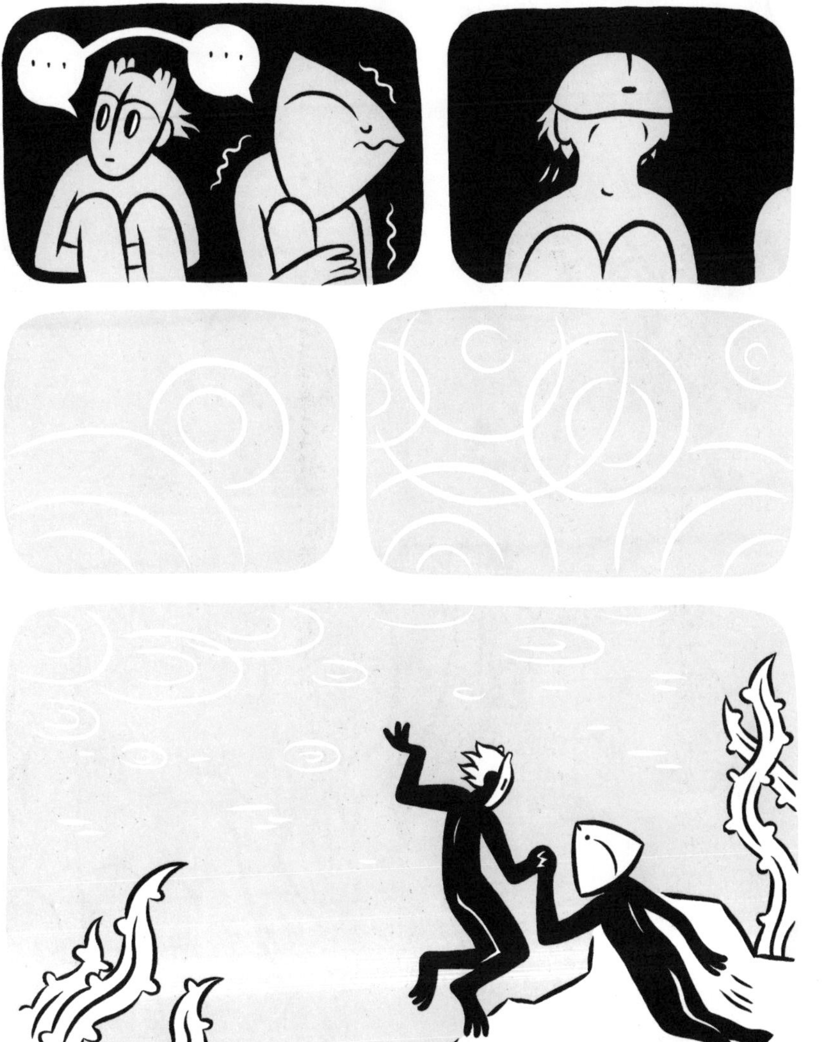
...
...

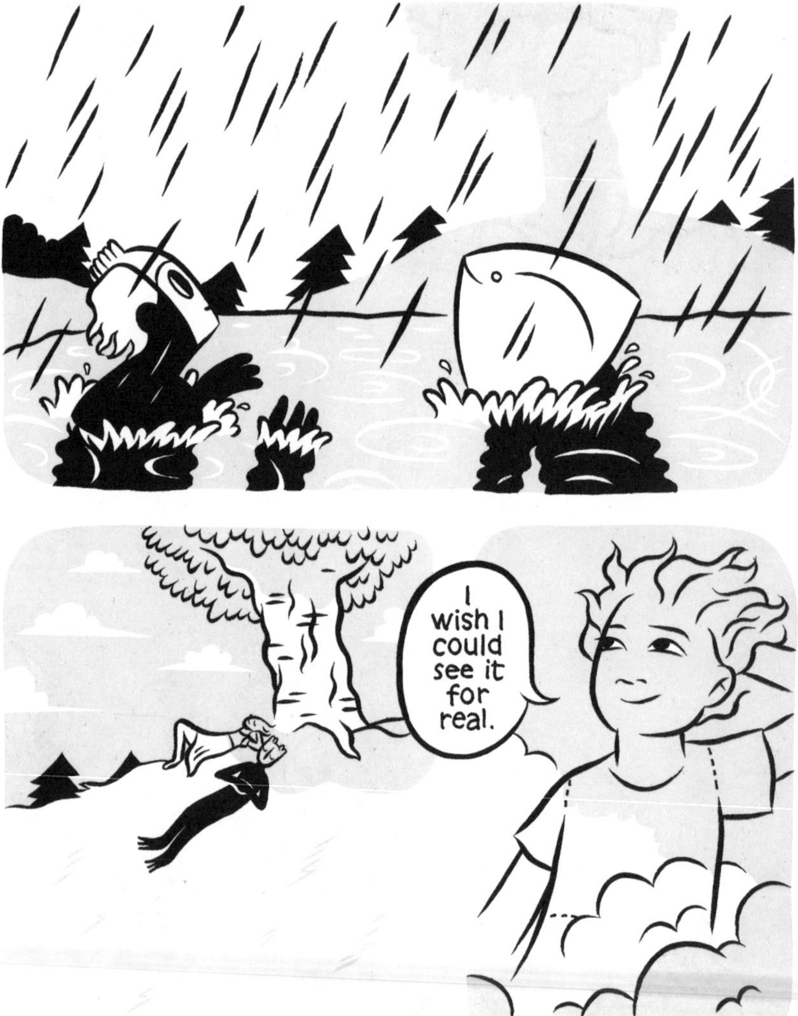
I wish I could see it for real.

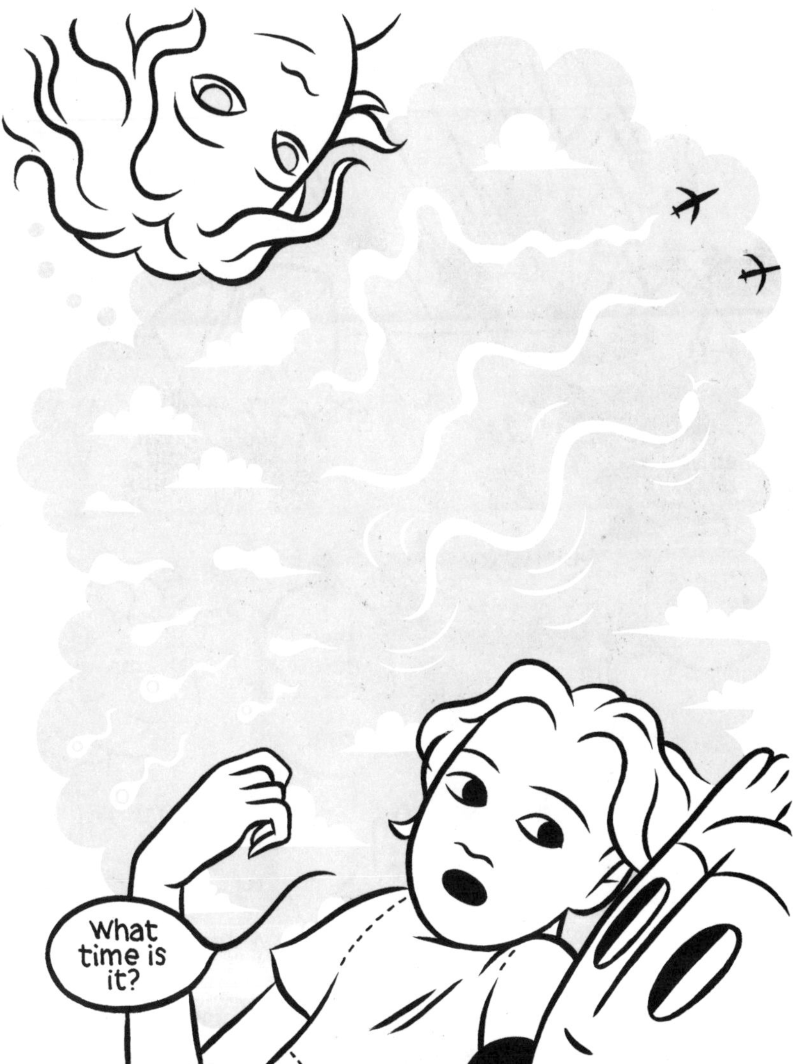
What time is it?

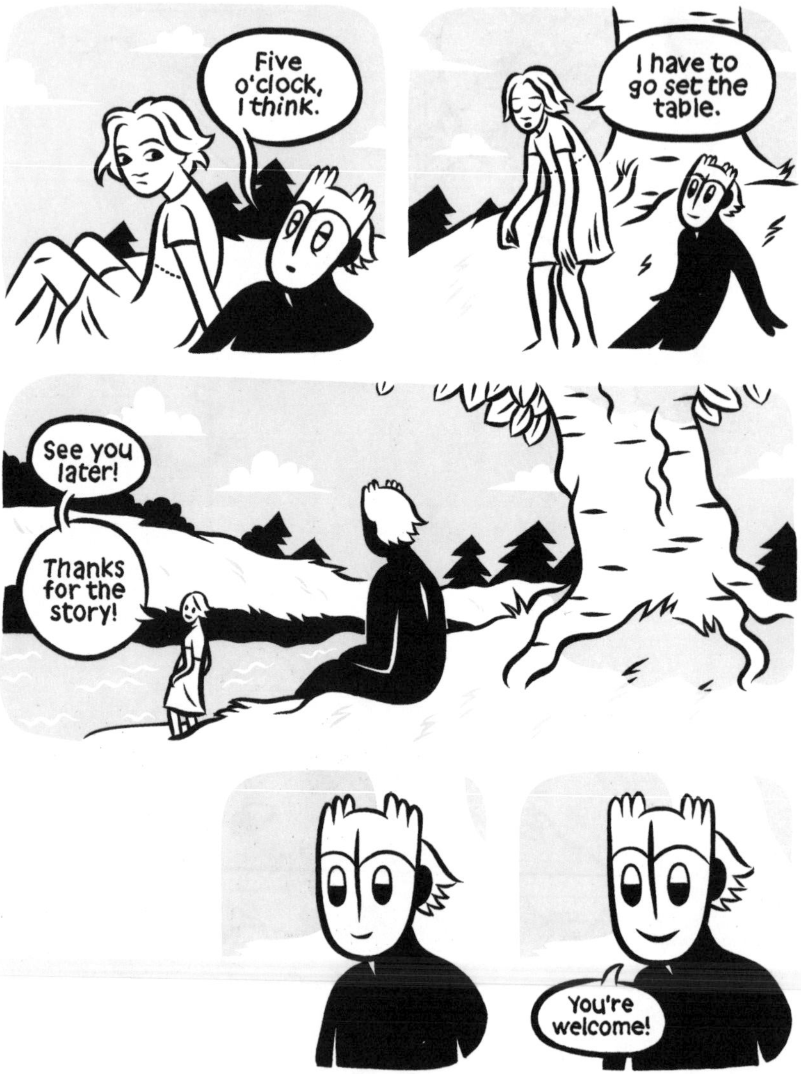
Five o'clock, I think.
I have to go set the table.
See you later!
Thanks for the story!
You're welcome!

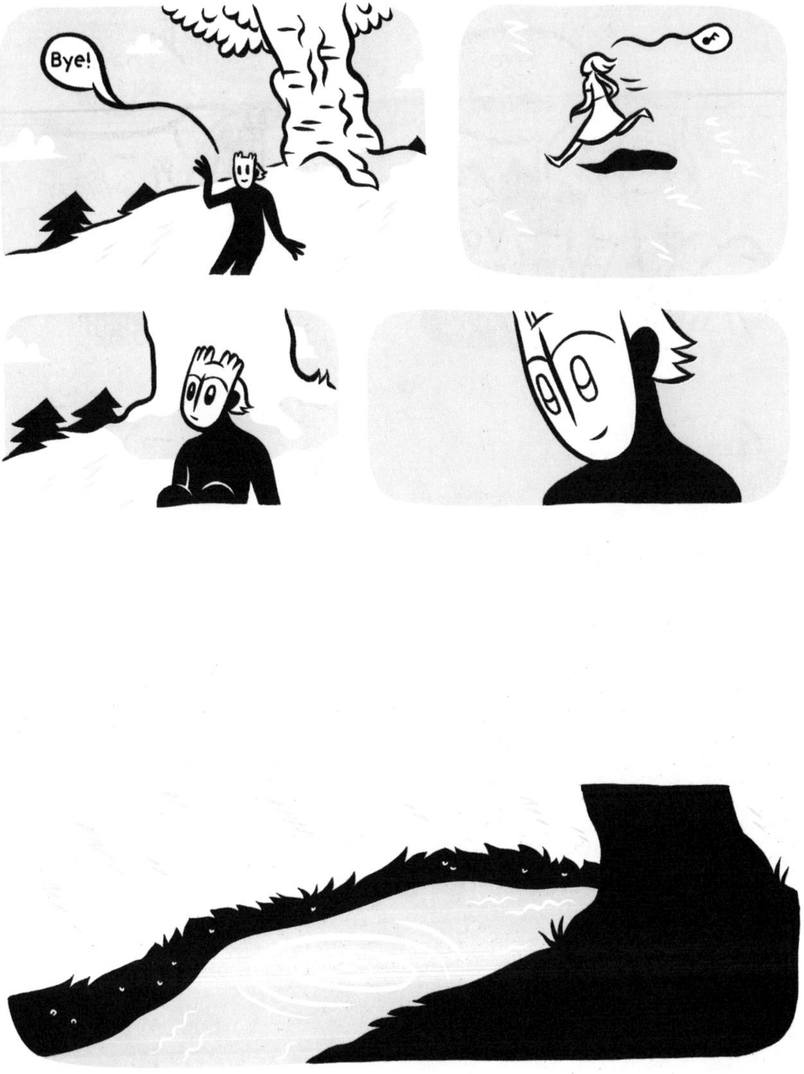
Bye!

She often returned to the creek, but it was a long time before Hailey saw Salamander again. Several years passed. New families moved into the neighborhood, and during summer the local children played epic games of Red Rover and Capture the Flag — but best of all was Hide and Seek.

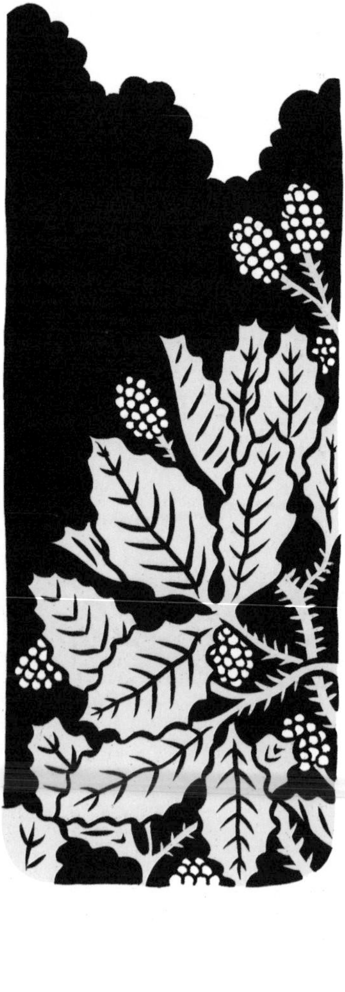
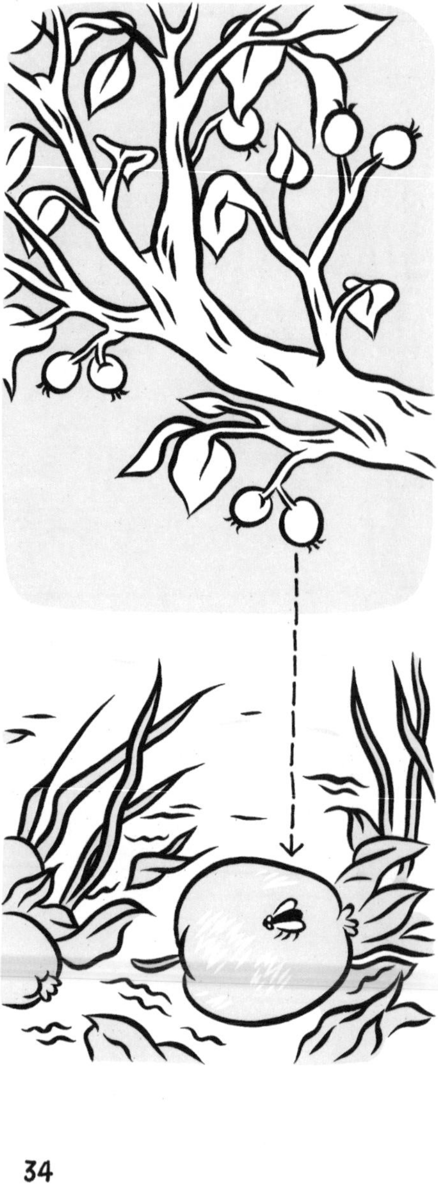

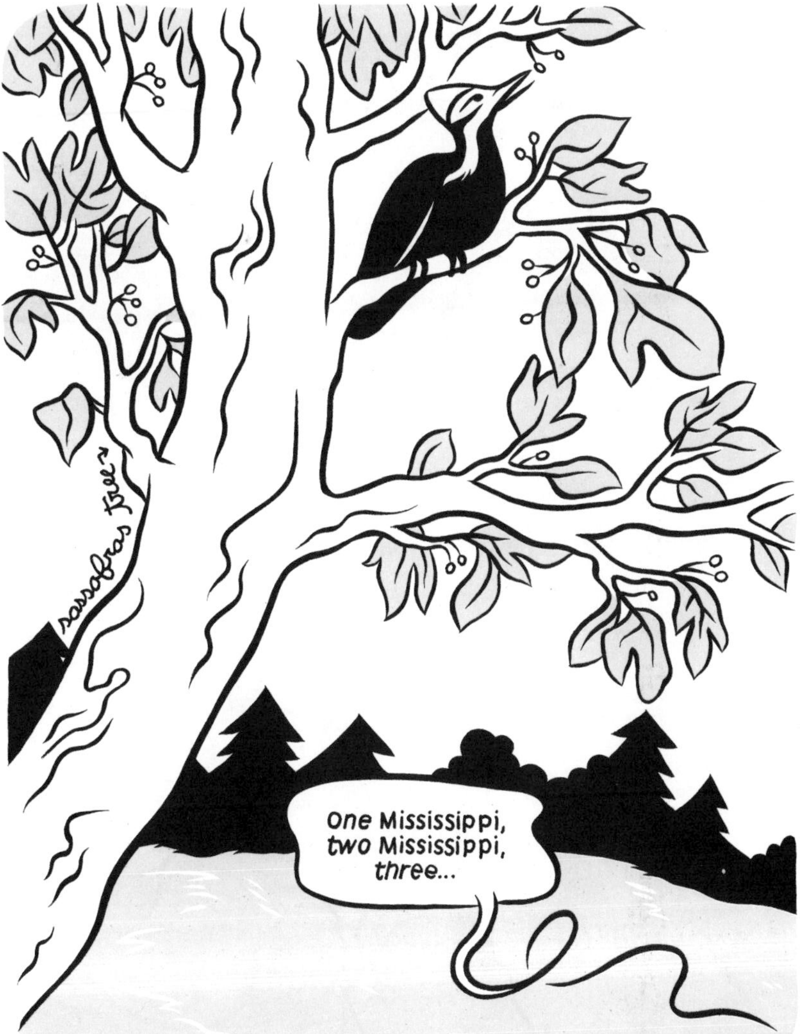
sassafras tree
One Mississippi, two Mississippi, three...

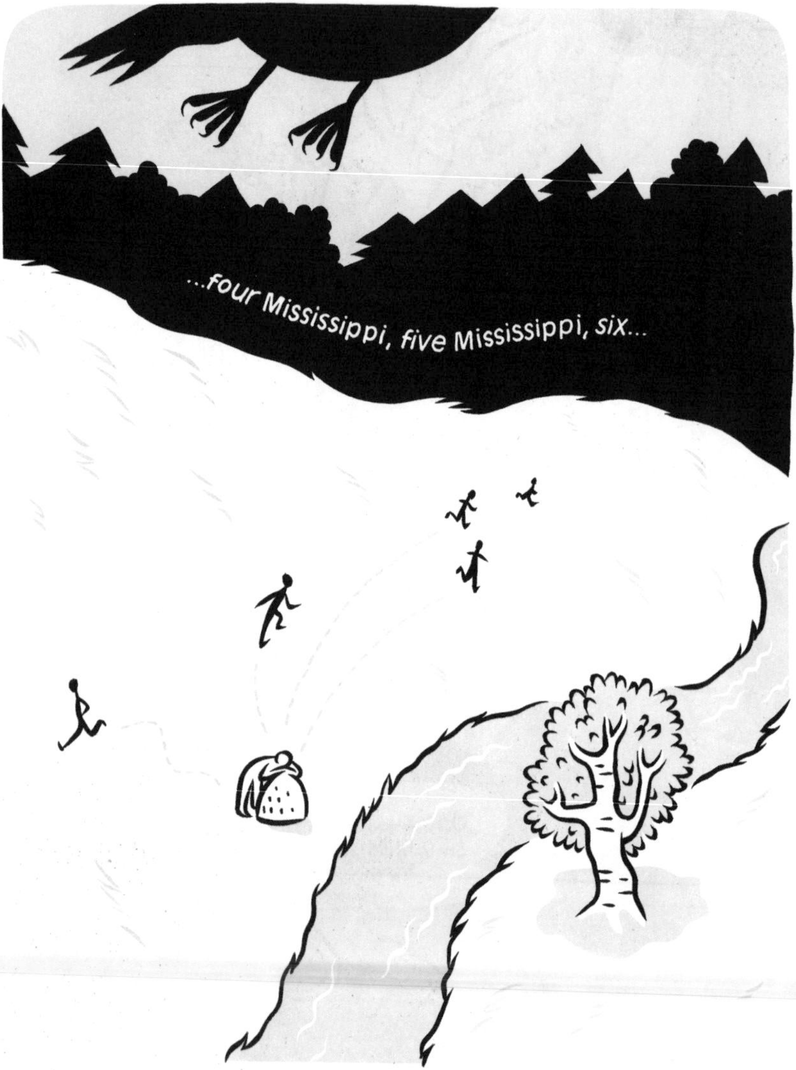
...four Mississippi, five Mississippi, six...

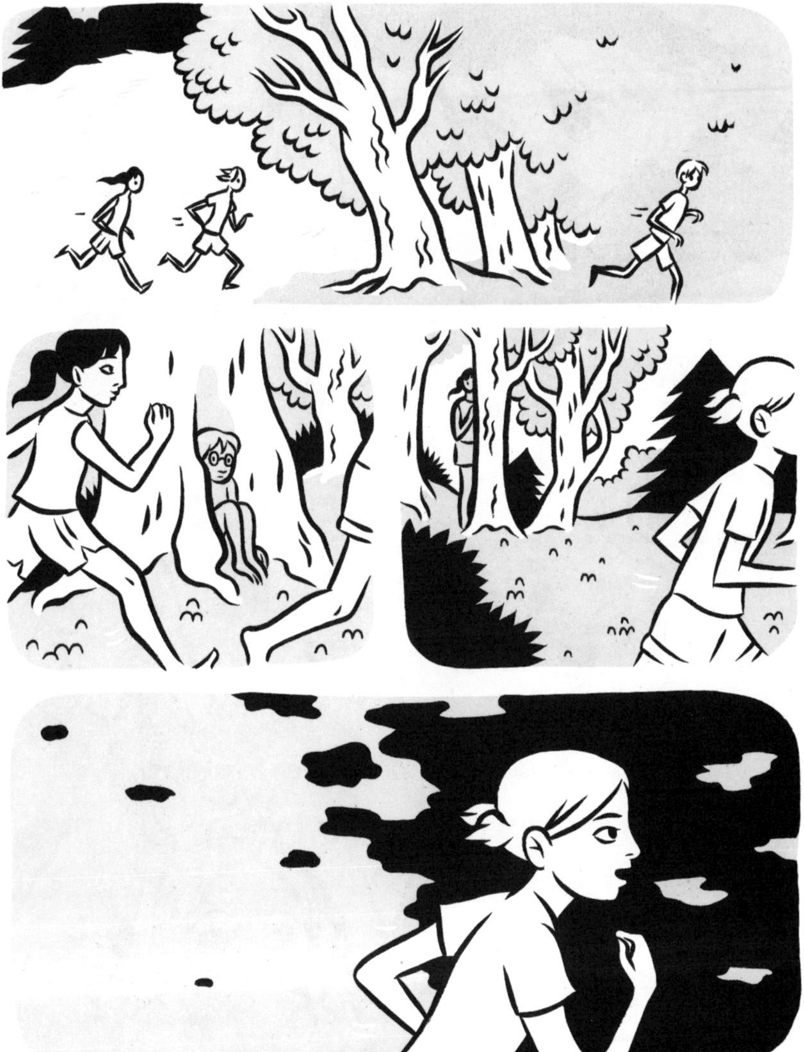

...*thirty-six* Mississippi, *thirty-seven* Mississippi...

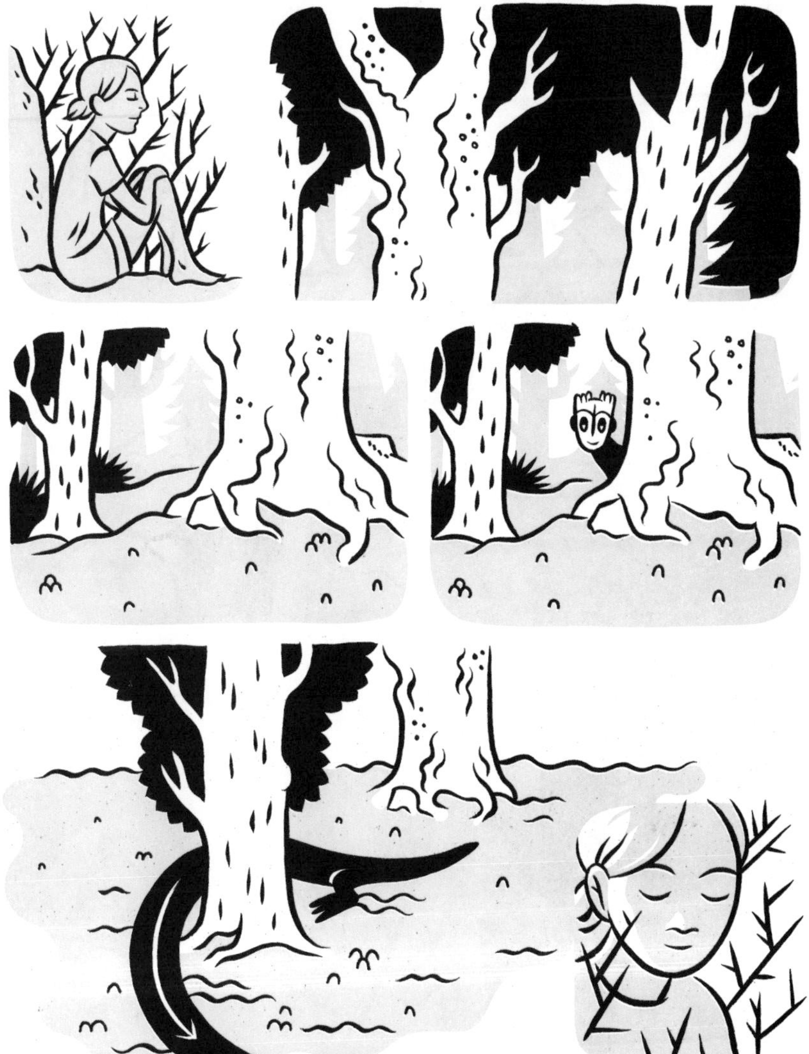

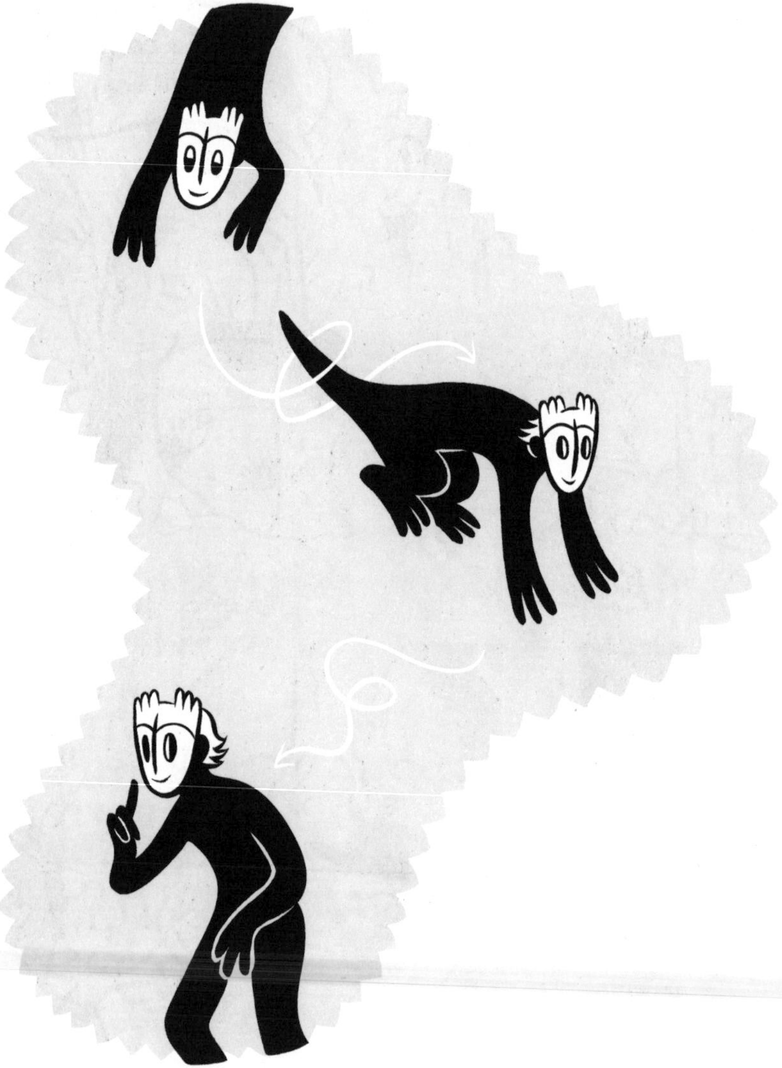

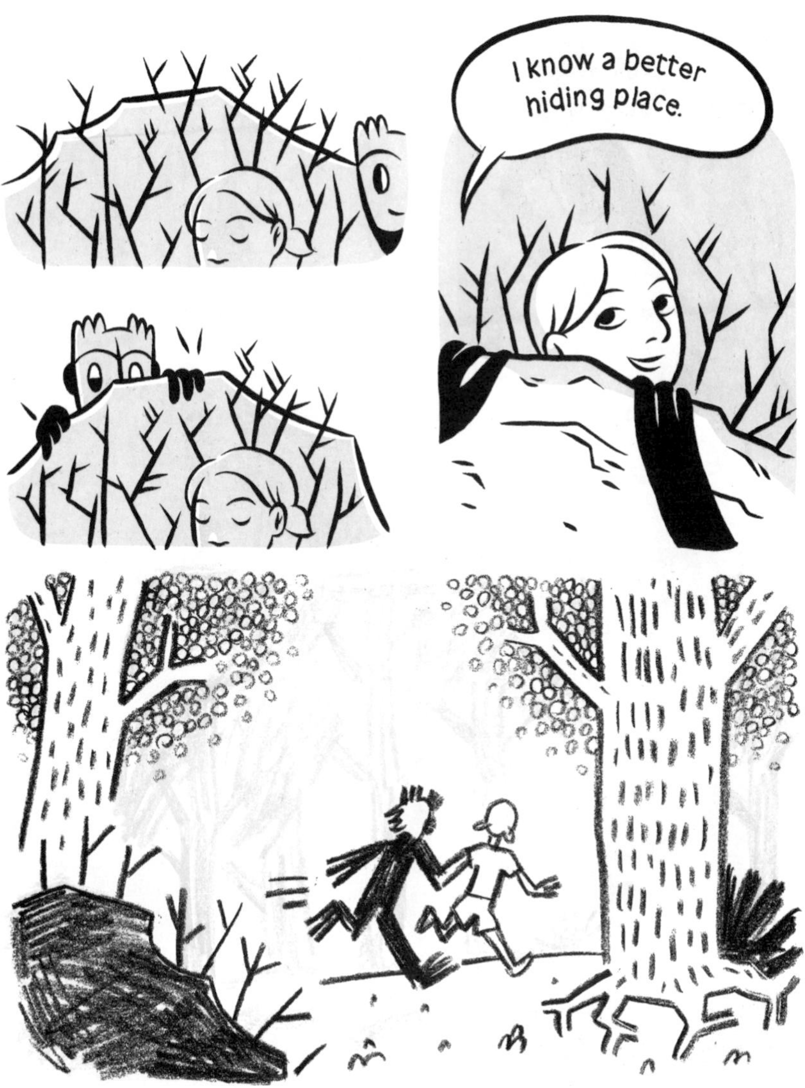
I know a better hiding place.

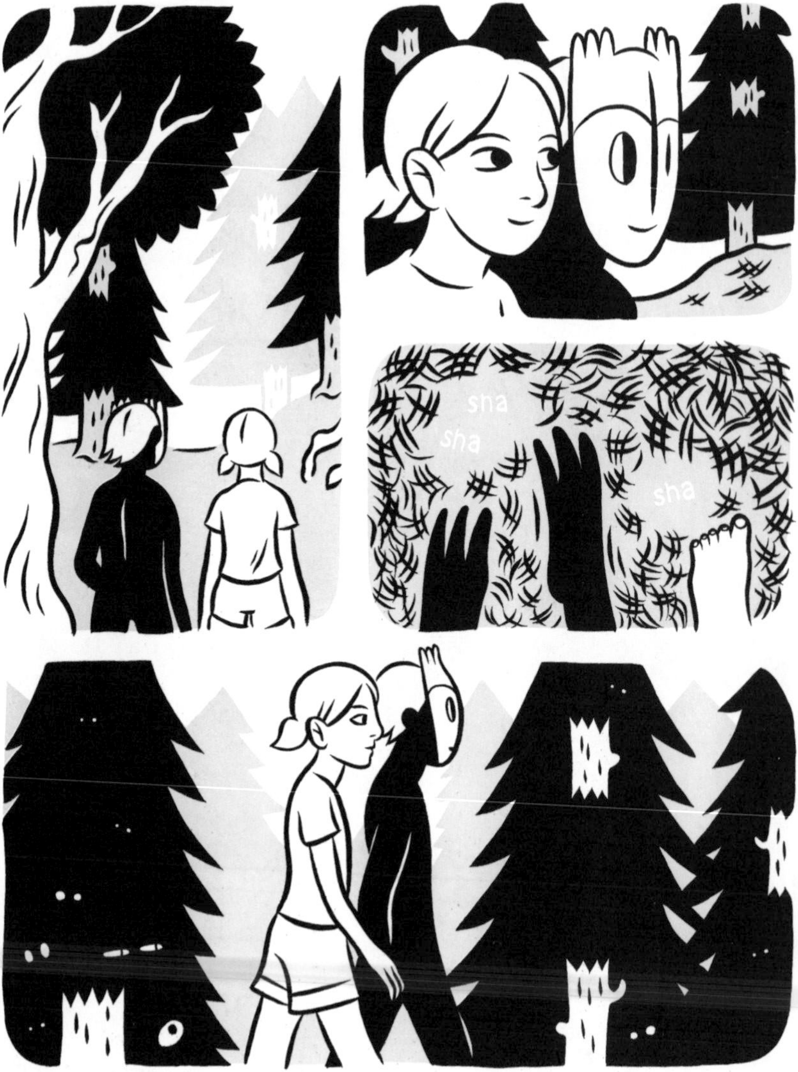
sha
sha
sha

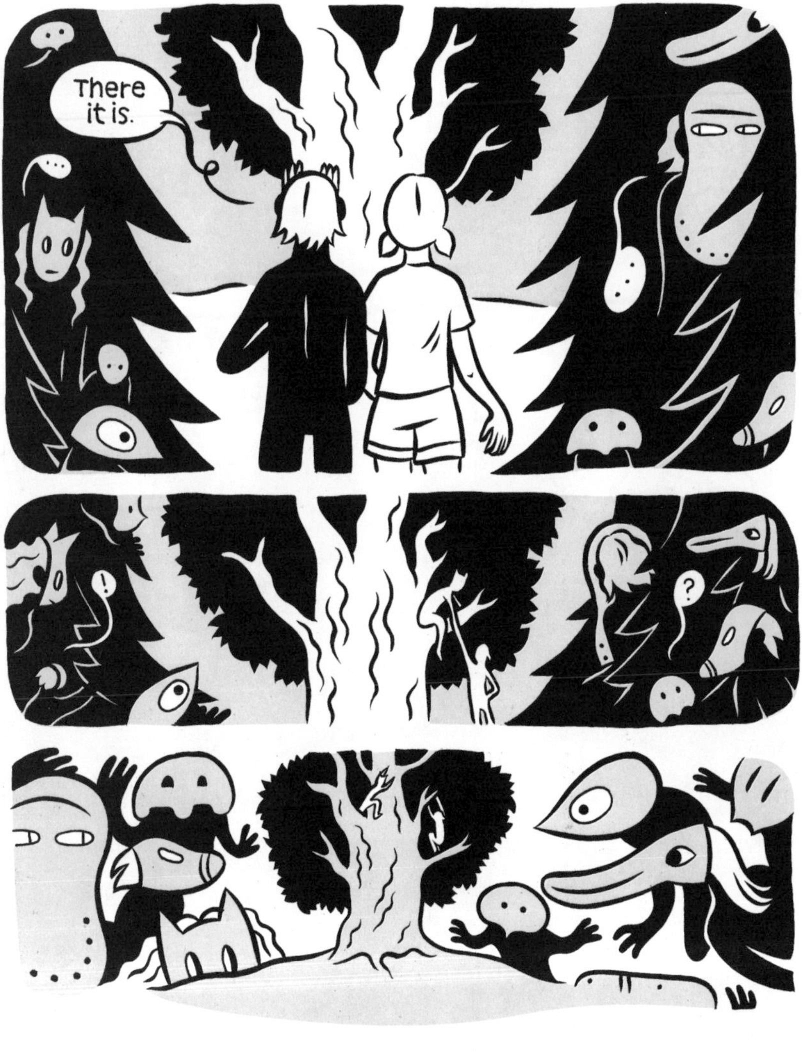
There it is.
!
?

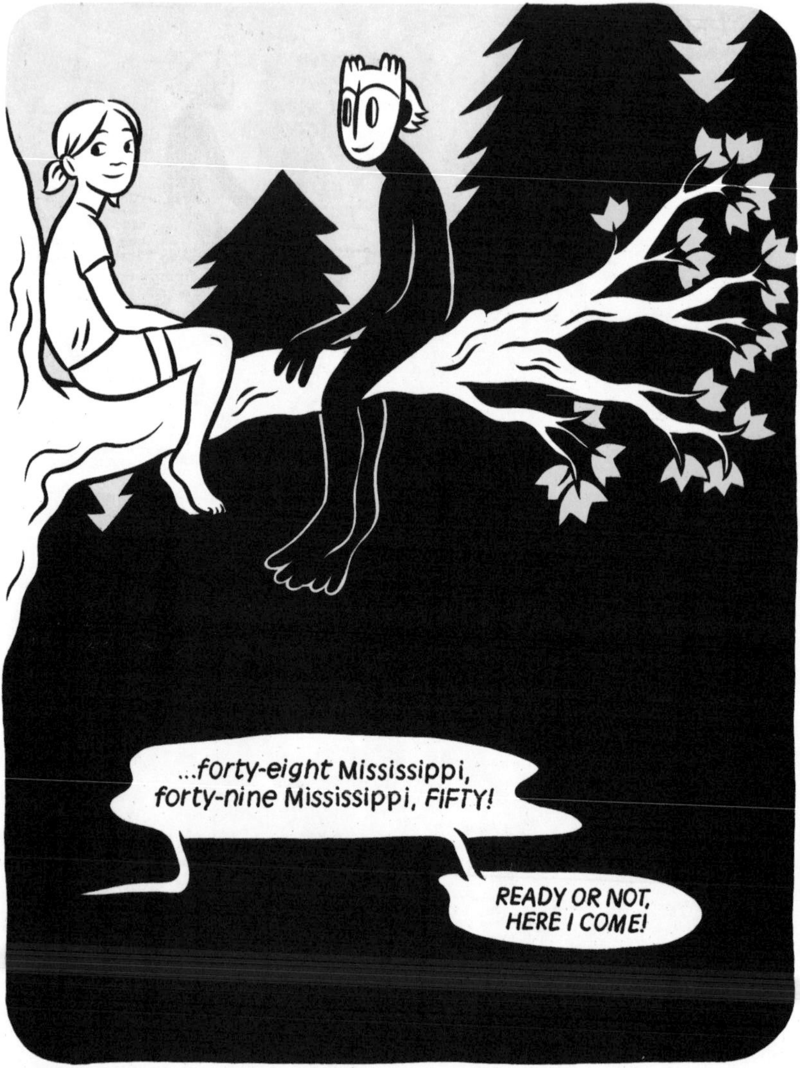
...forty-eight Mississippi,
forty-nine Mississippi, FIFTY!
READY OR NOT,
HERE I COME!

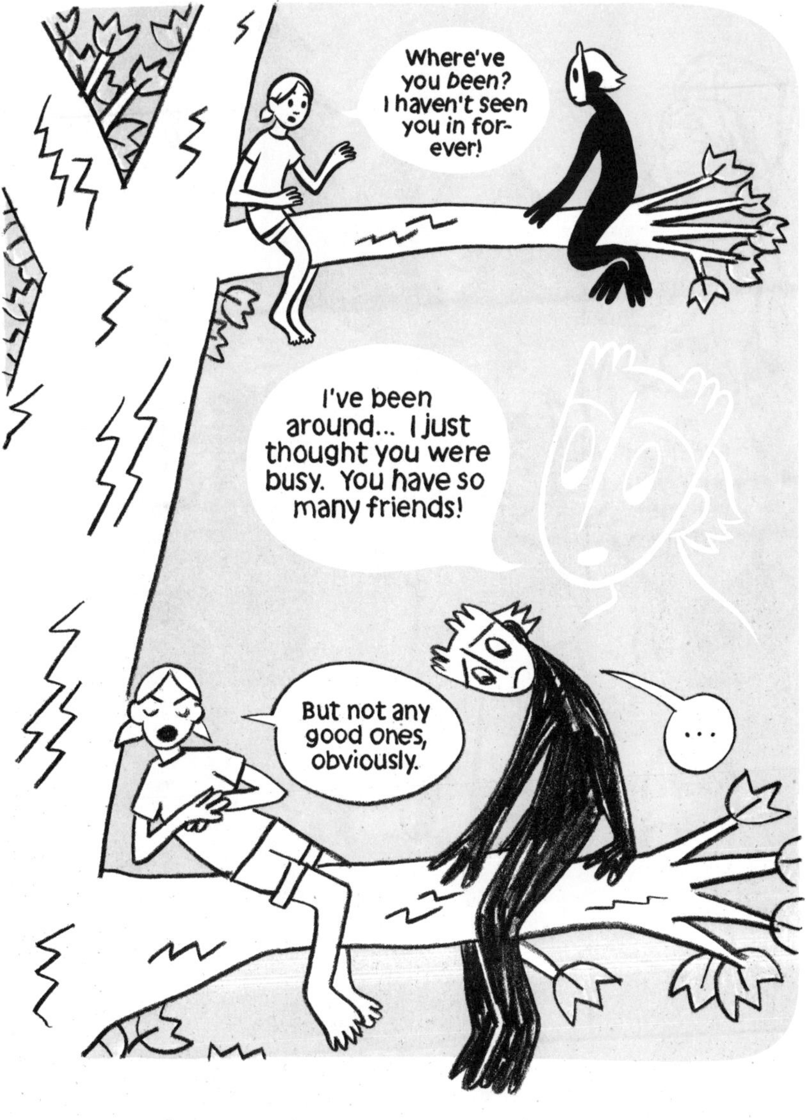
Where've you *been*? I haven't seen you in for-ever!
I've been around... I just thought you were busy. You have so many friends!
But not any good ones, obviously.
...

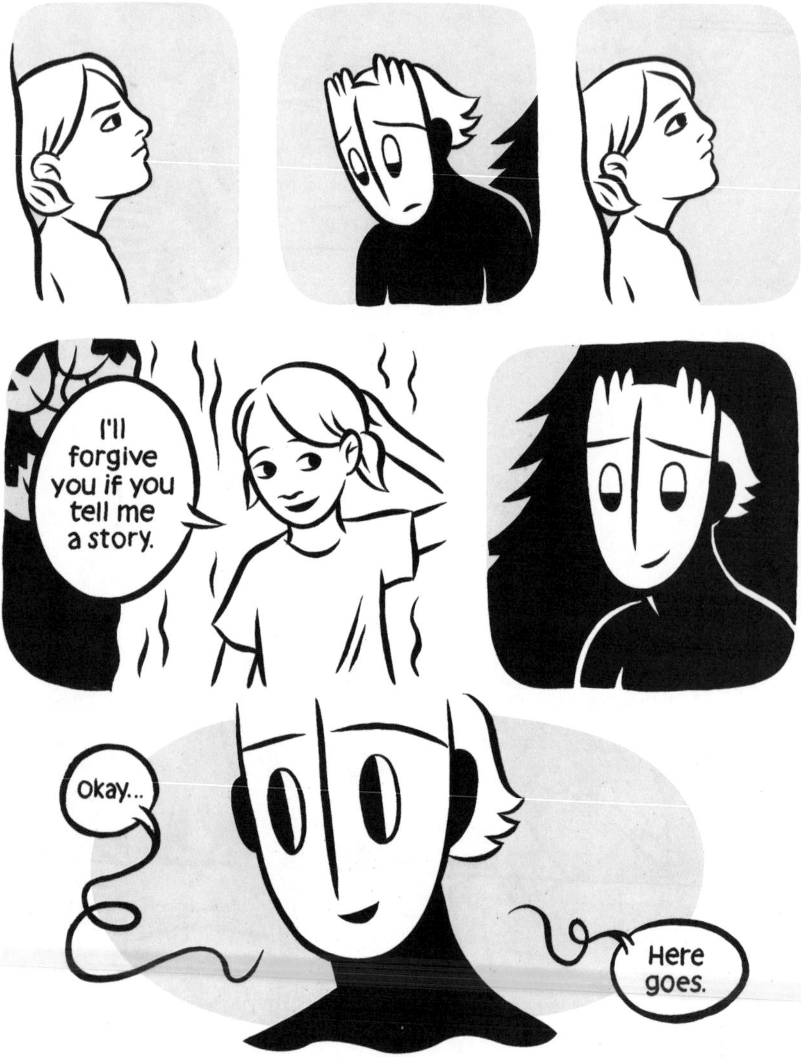
I'll forgive you if you tell me a story.
Okay...
Here goes.

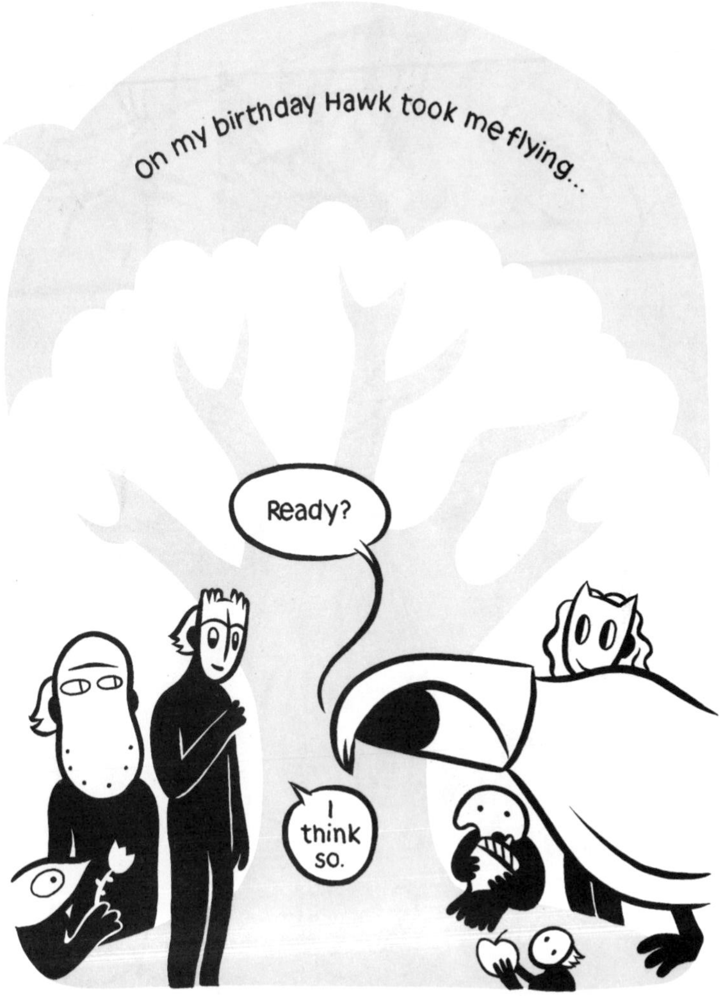
On my birthday Hawk took me flying...
Ready?
I think so.

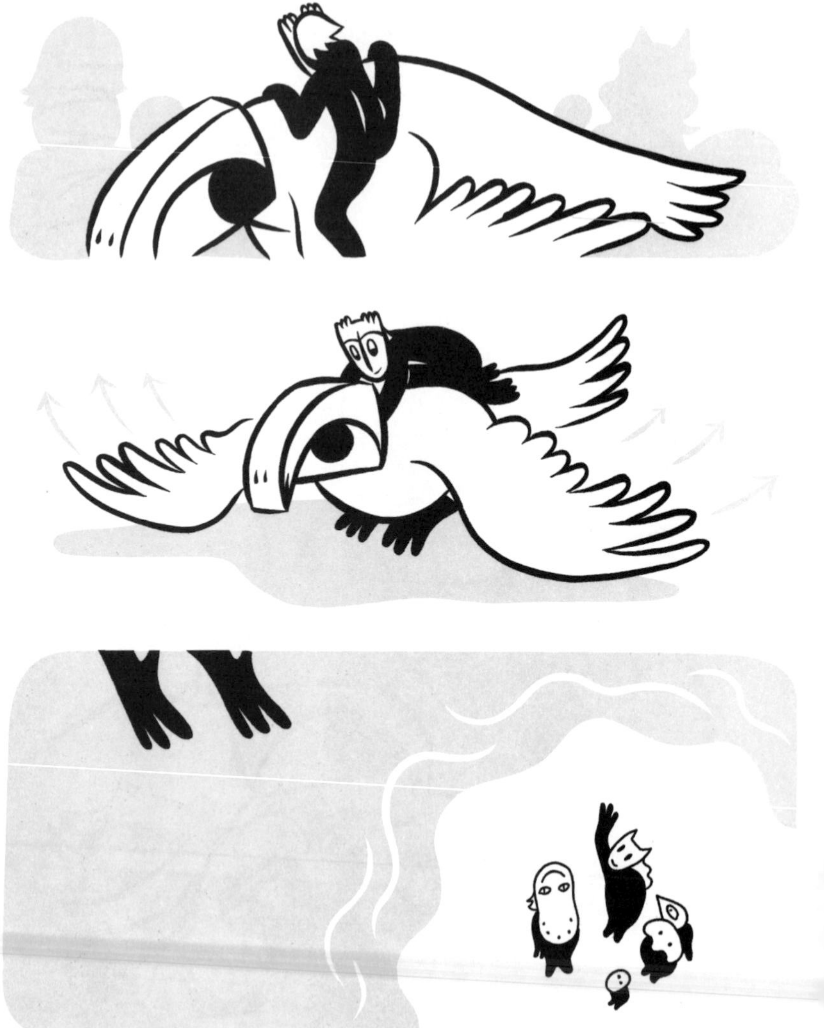

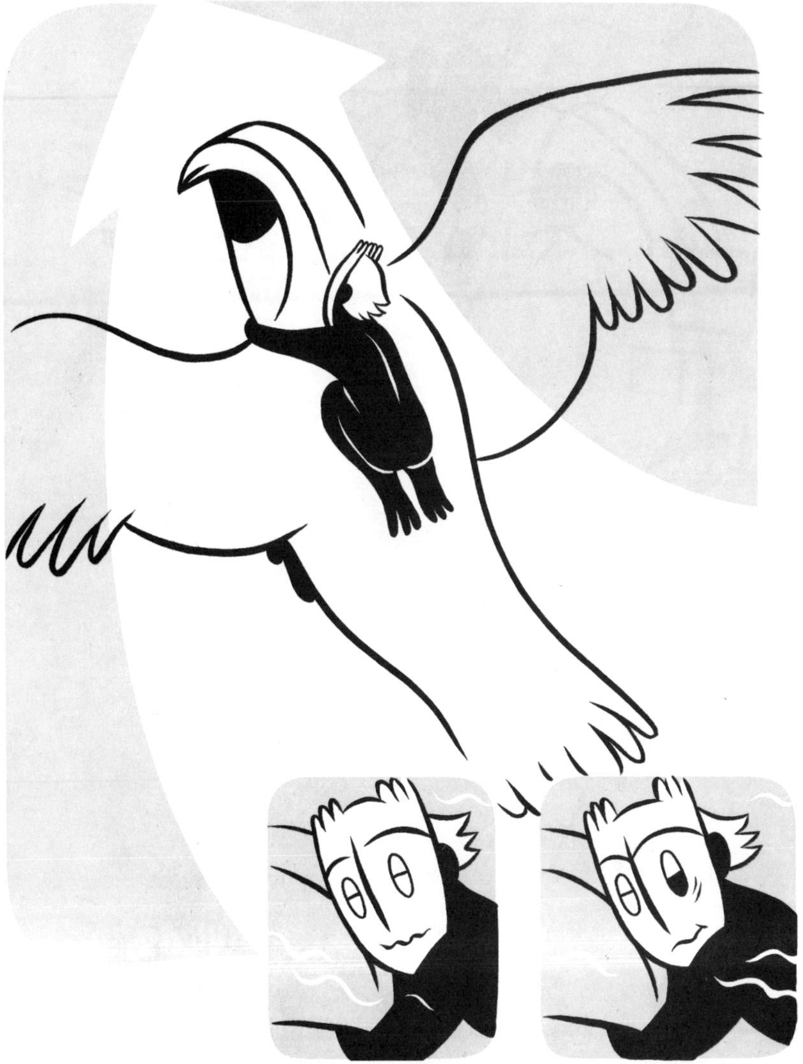

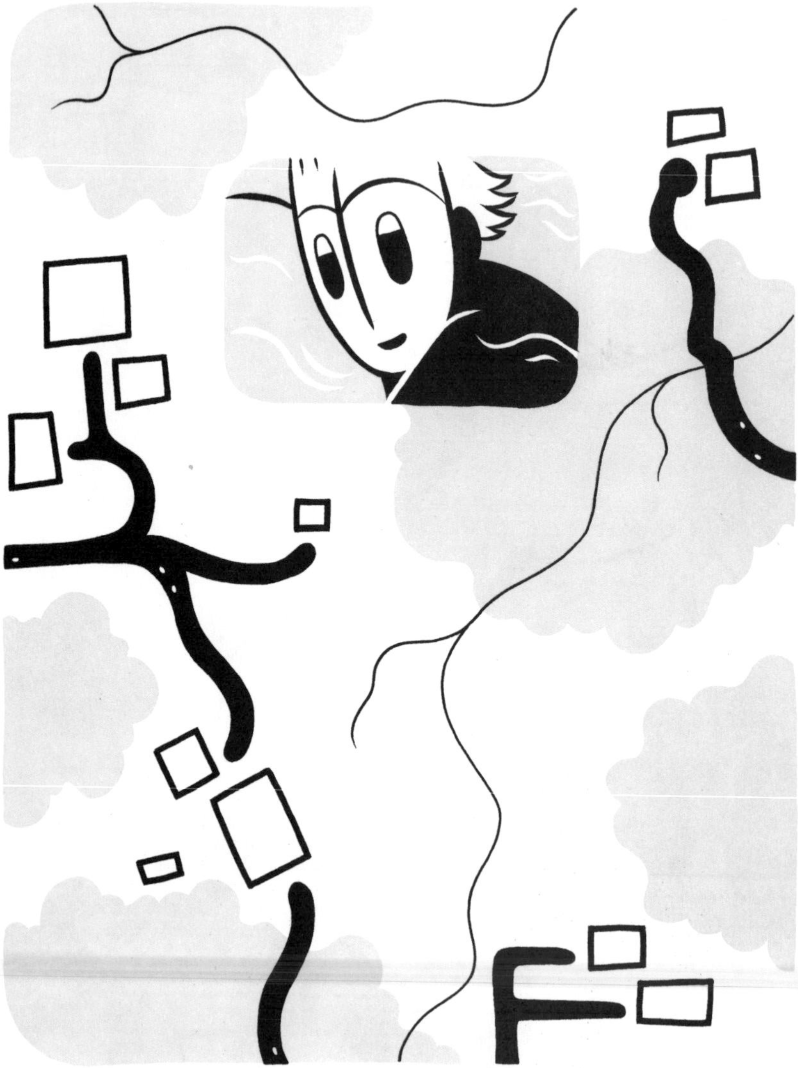

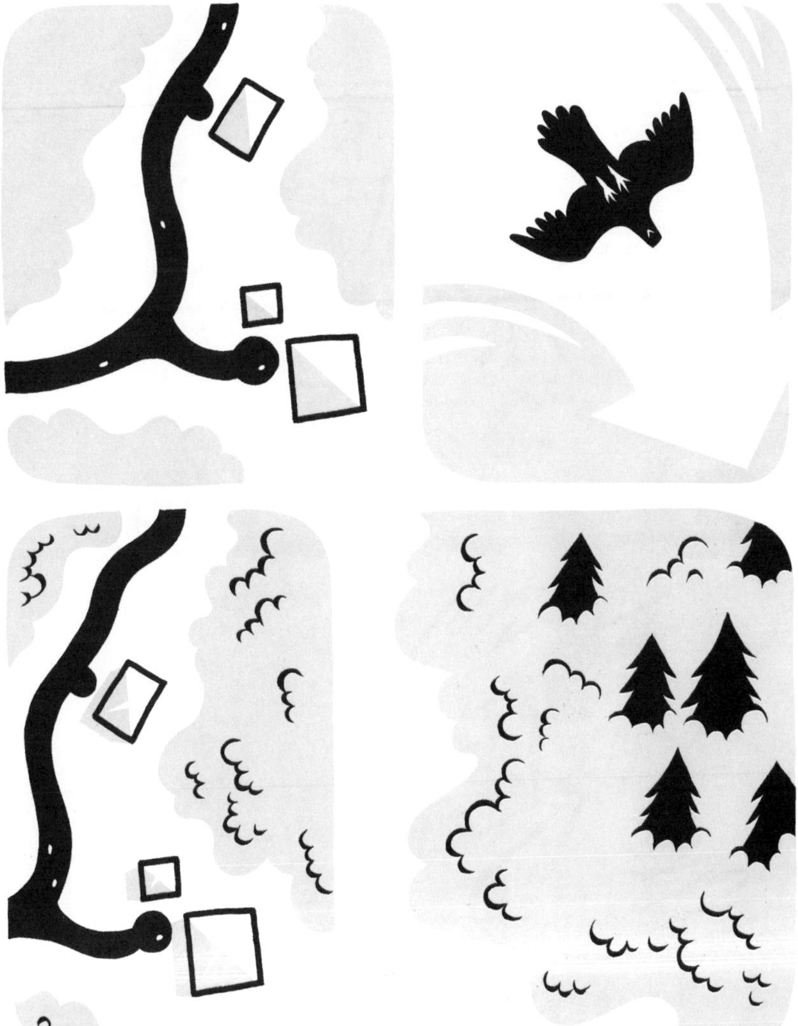

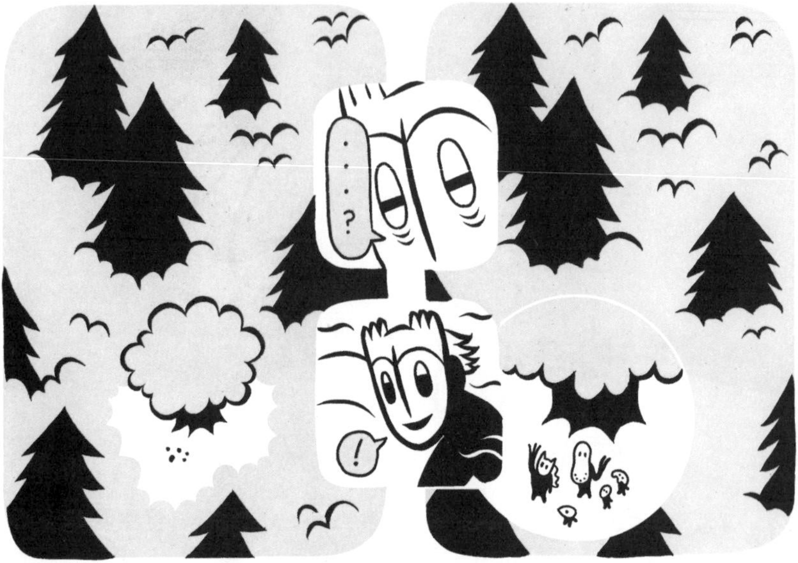
. . . ?
!

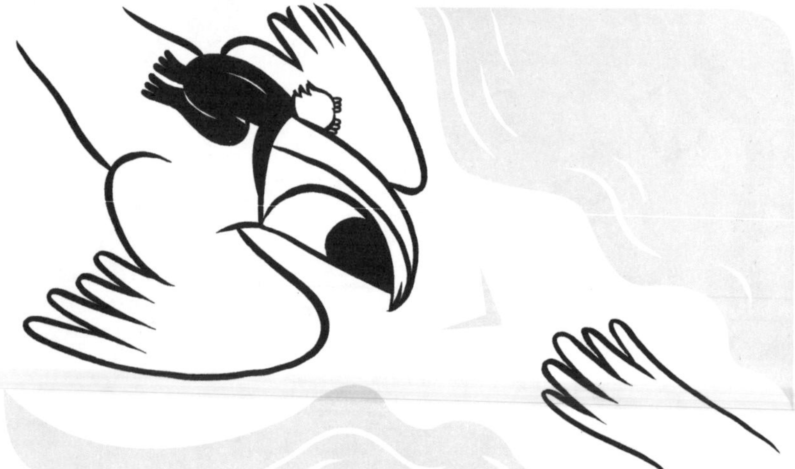

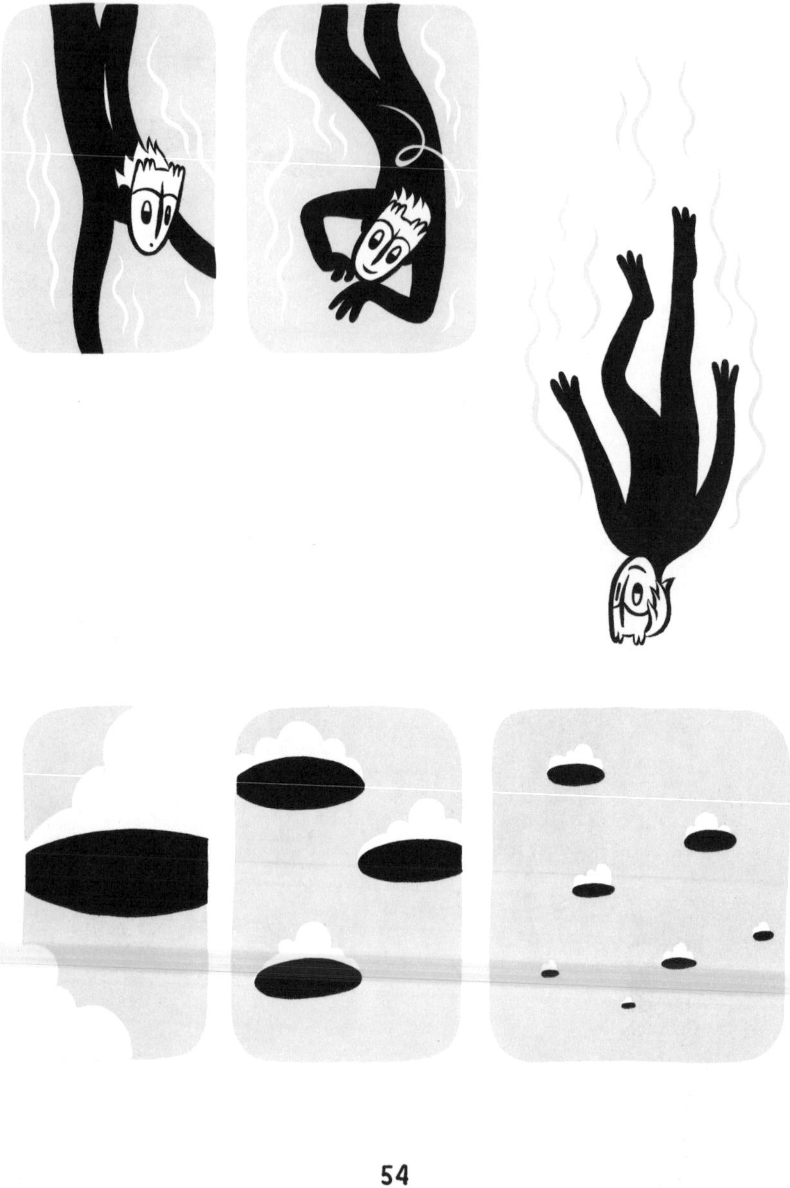

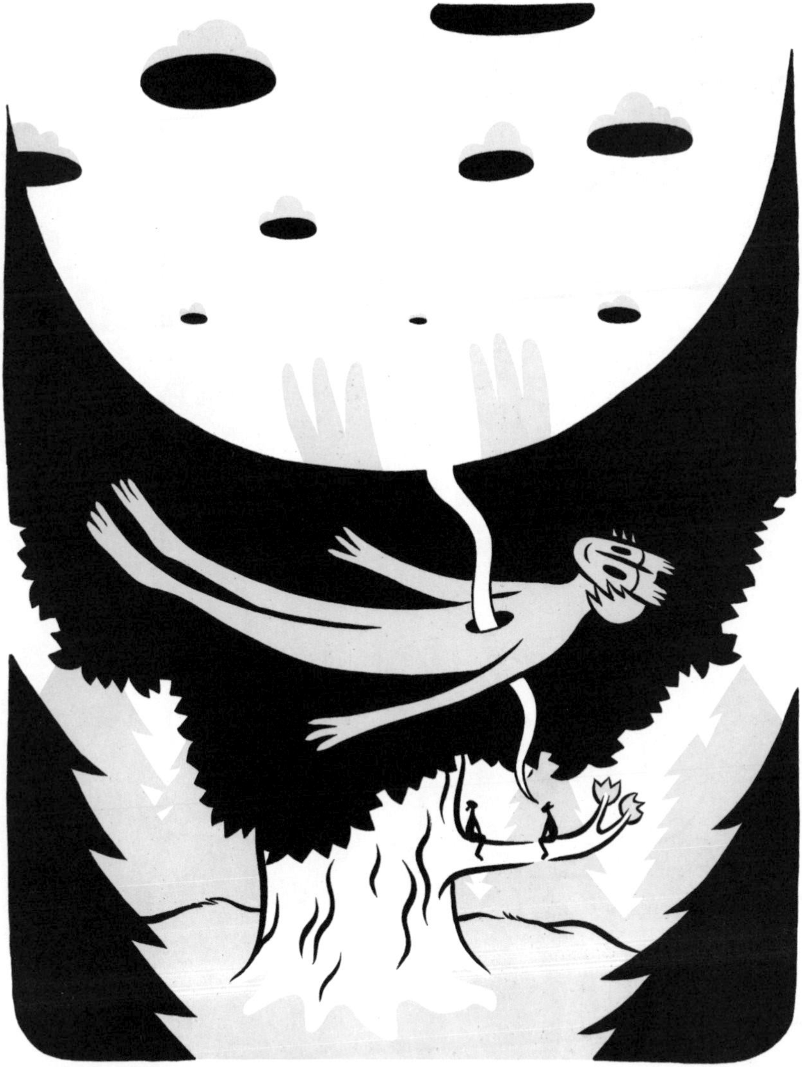

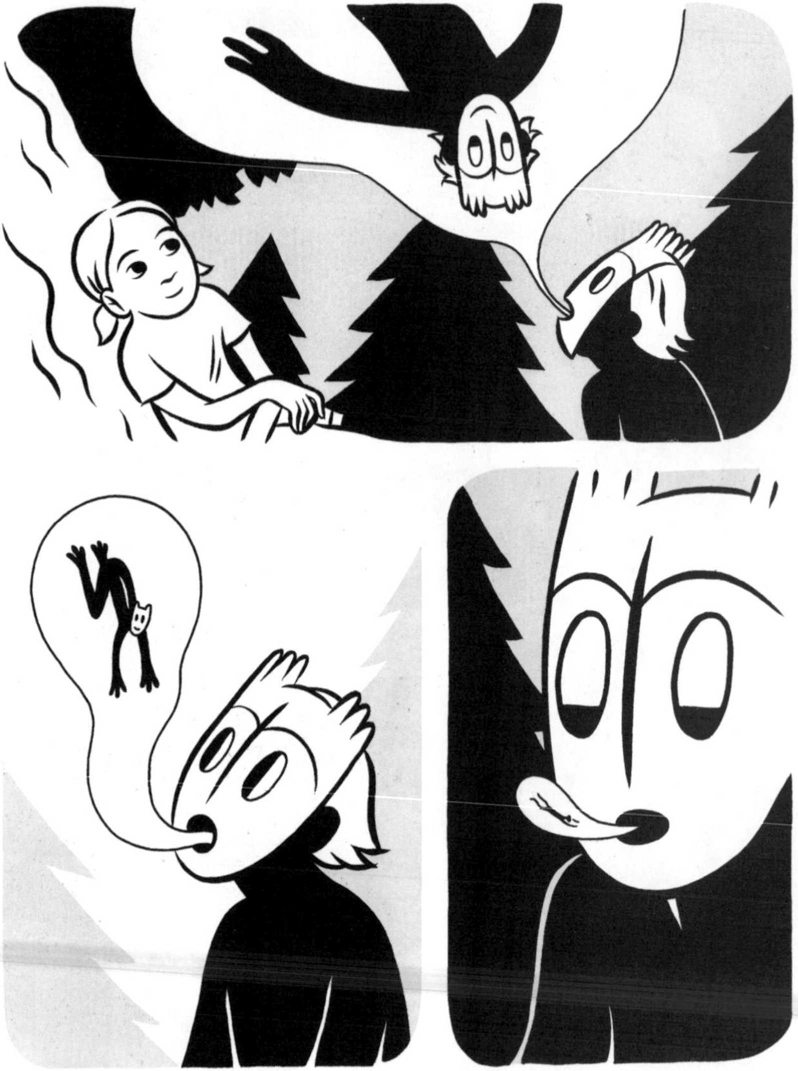

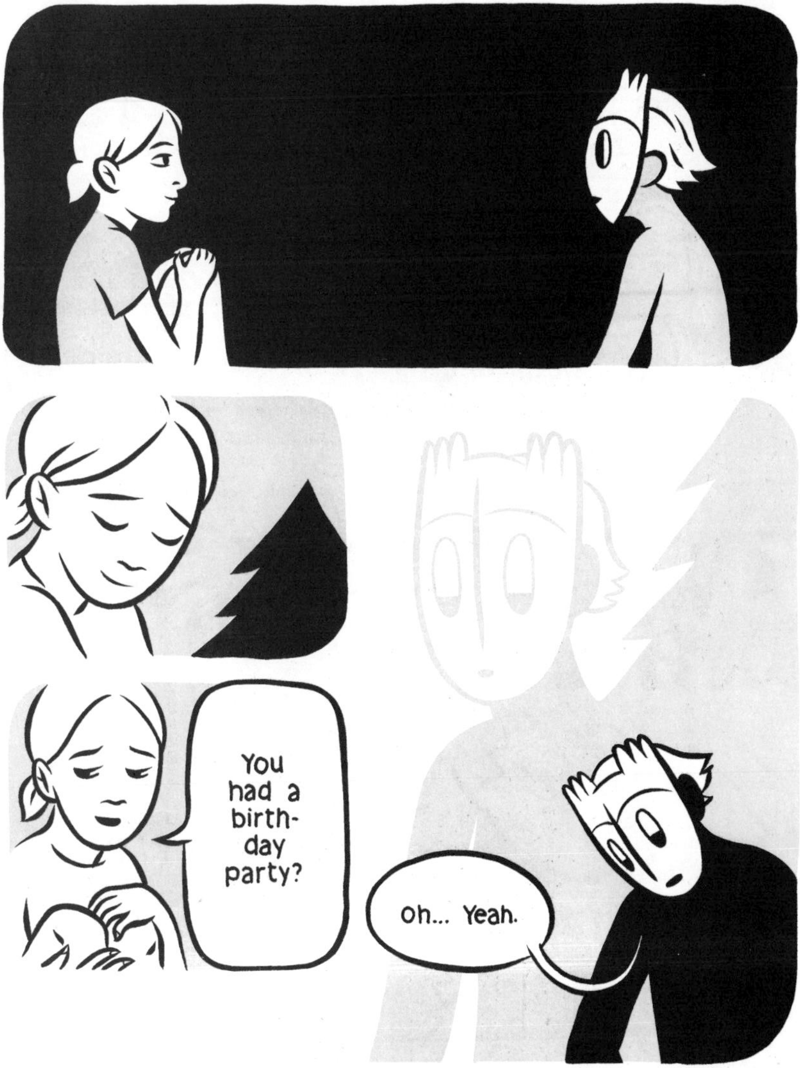
You had a birth-day party?
Oh... Yeah.

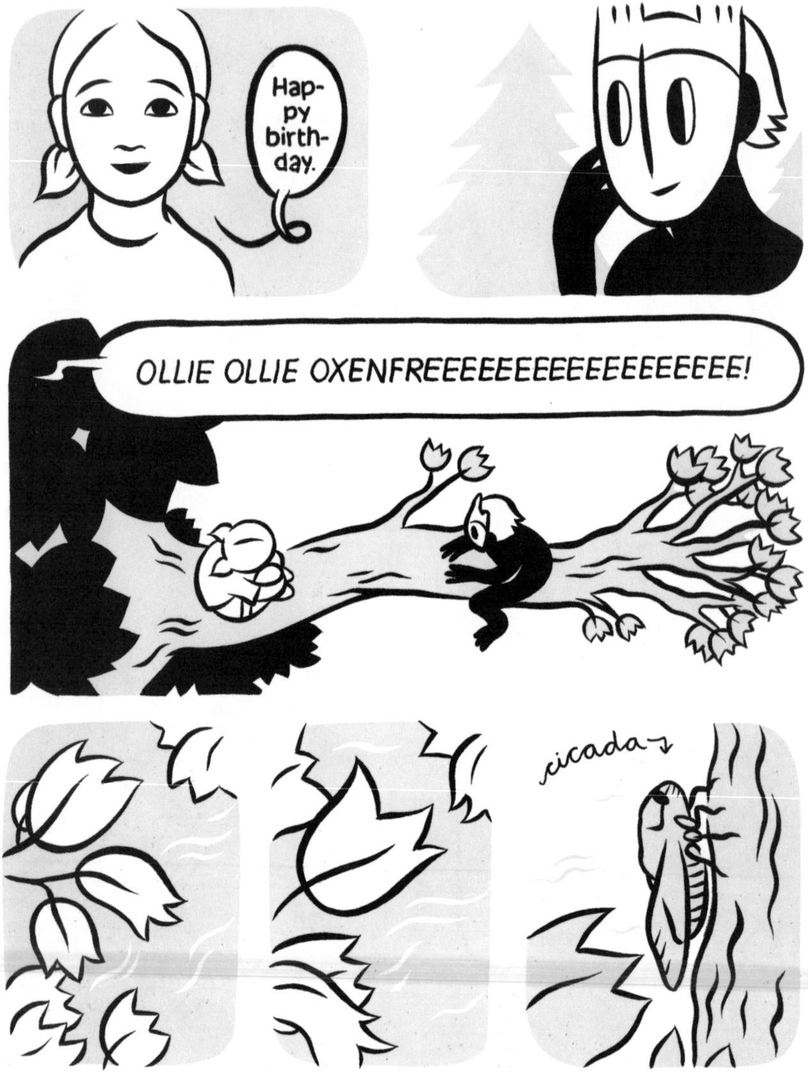
Hap-py birth-day.
OLLIE OLLIE OXENFREEEEEEEEEEEEEEEEEEEE!
cicada

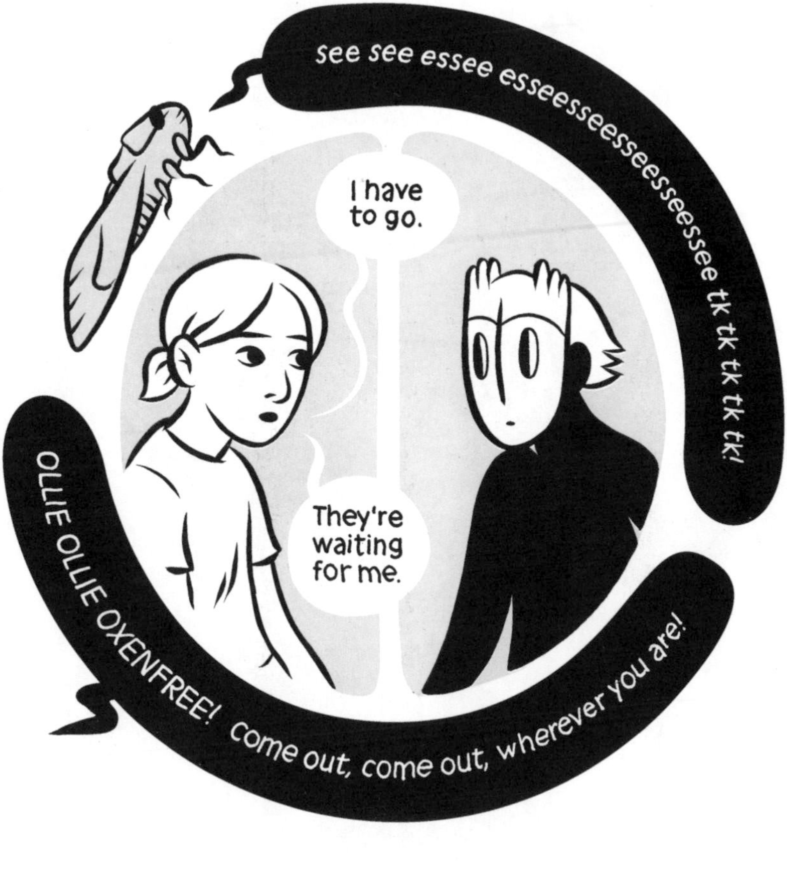
see see essee esseesseesseesseesseessee tk tk tk tk tk!
I have to go.
They're waiting for me.
OLLIE OLLIE OXENFREE! come out, come out, wherever you are!

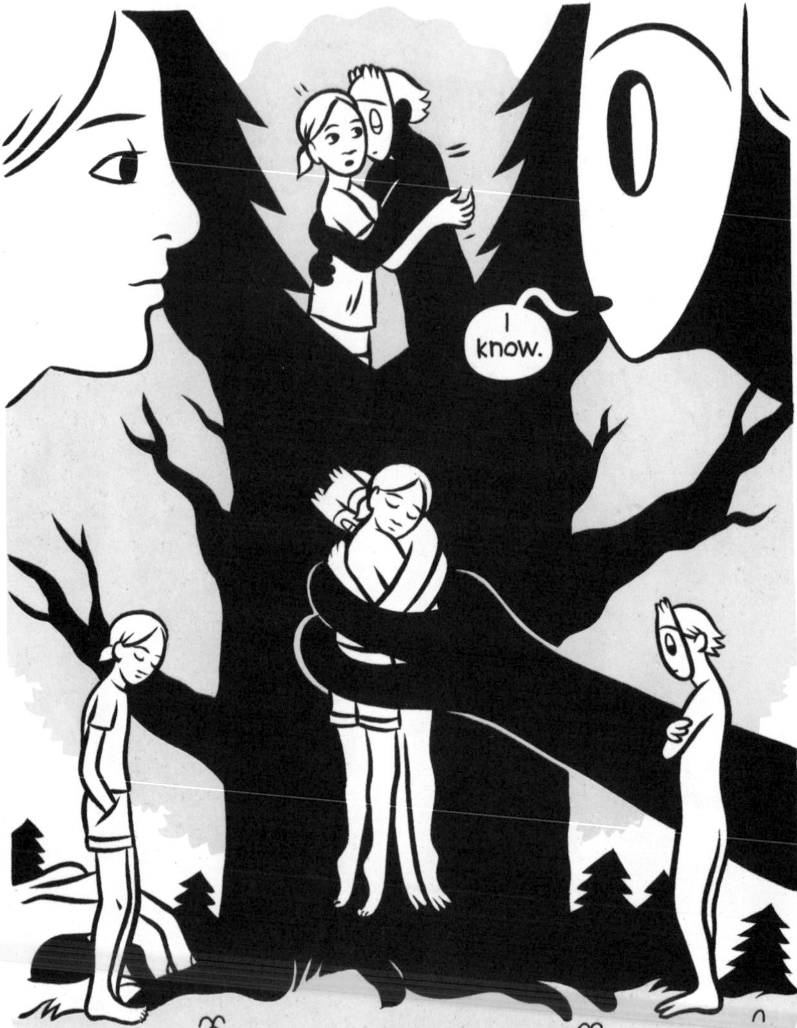
I know.

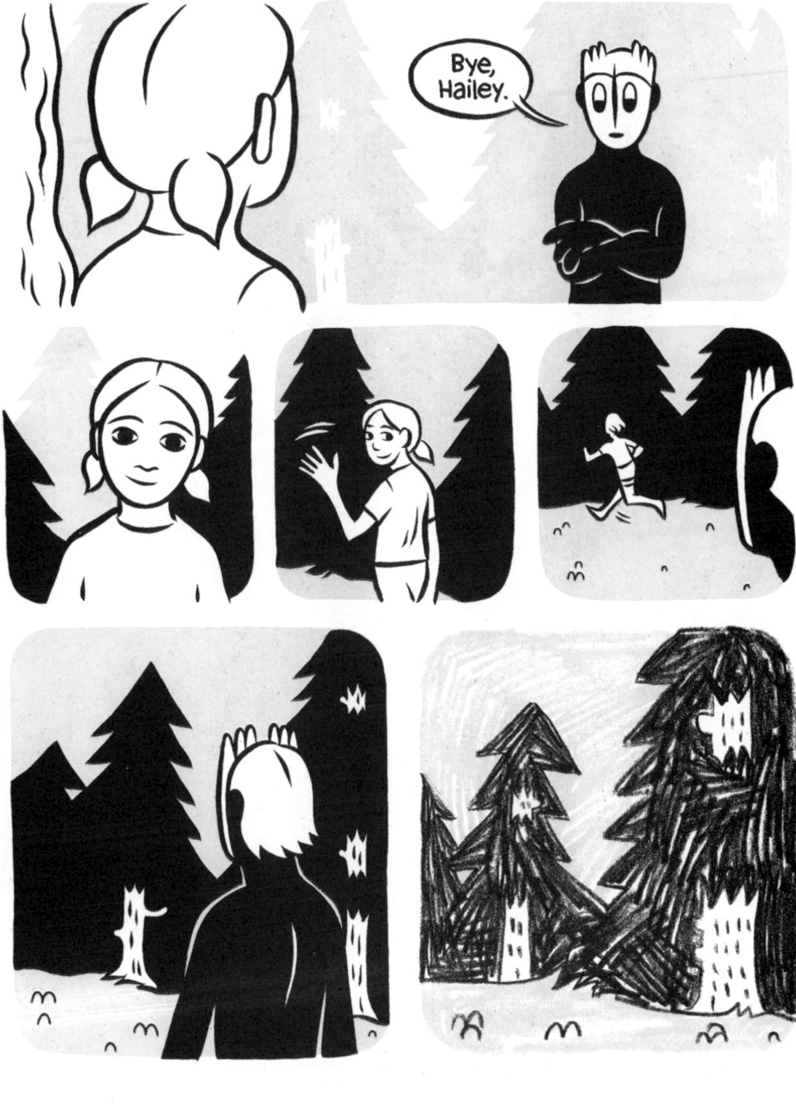
Bye, Hailey.

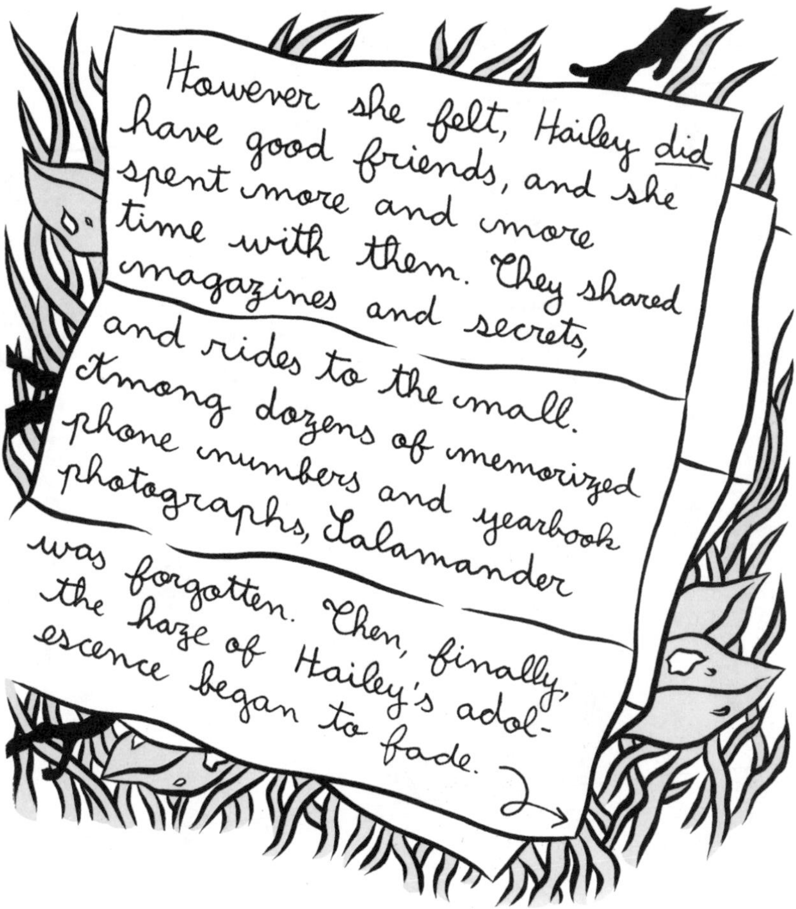

However she felt, Hailey *did* have good friends, and she spent more and more time with them. They shared magazines and secrets, and rides to the mall. Among dozens of memorized phone numbers and yearbook photographs, Salamander was forgotten. Then, finally, the haze of Hailey's adolescence began to fade.

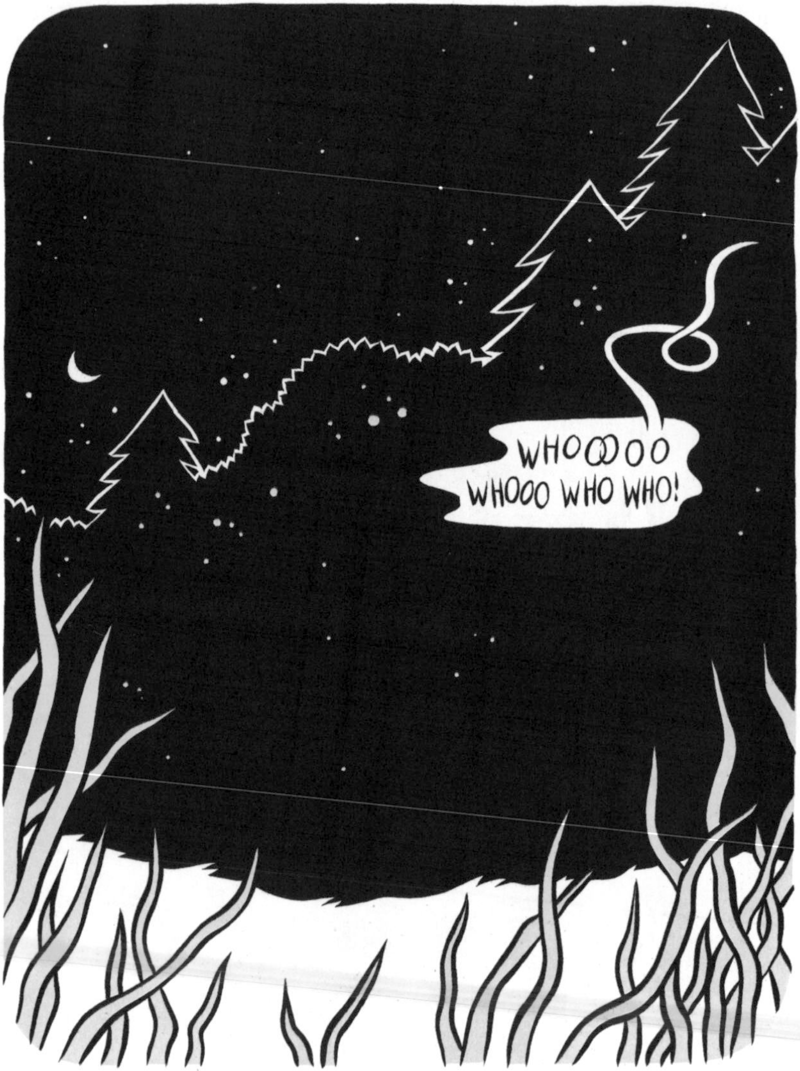
WHOOOOO
WHOOO WHO WHO!

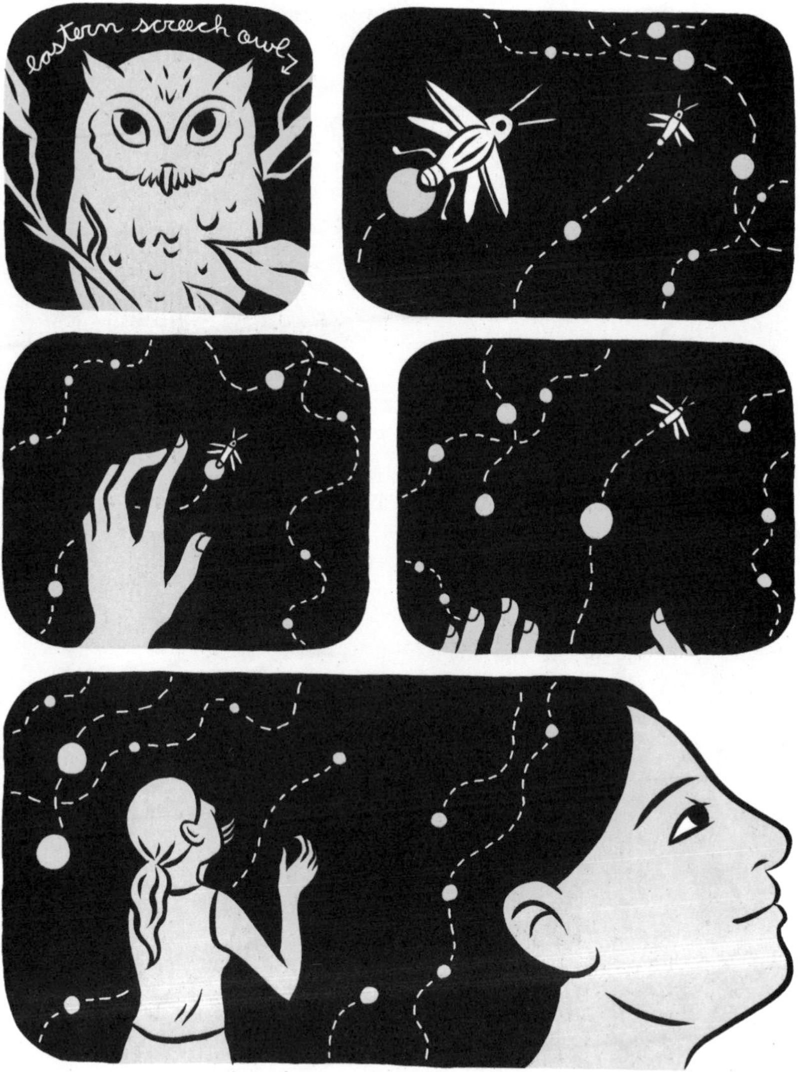
eastern screech owl

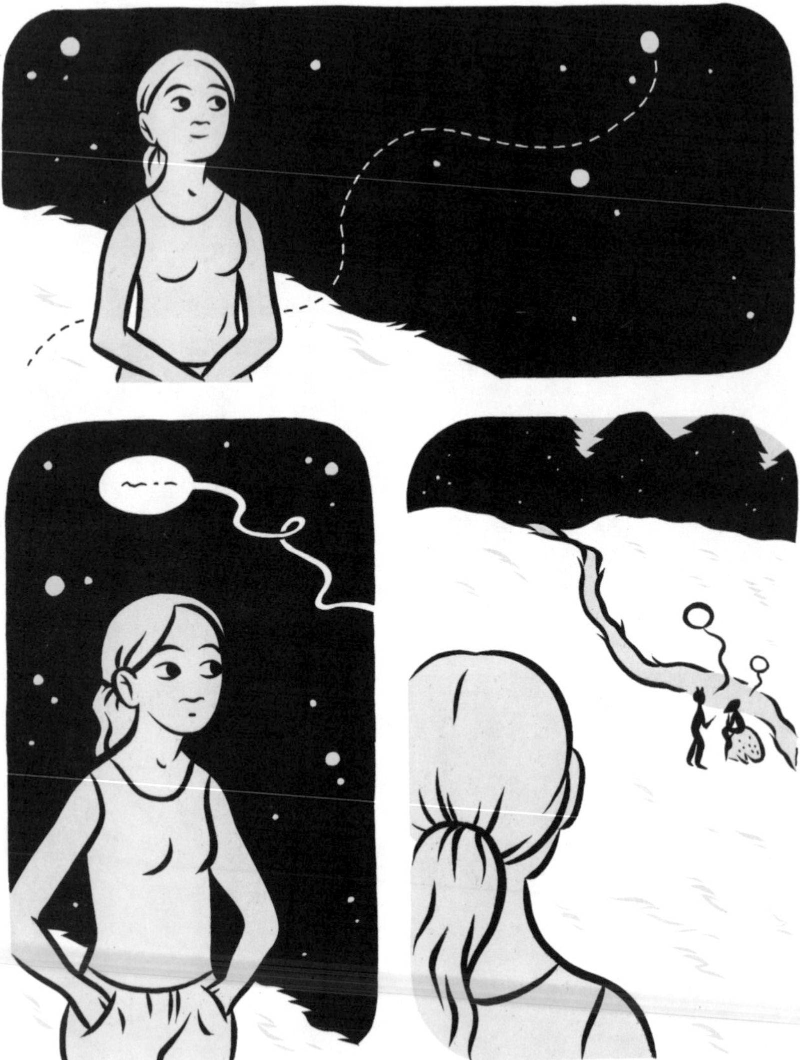

hee hee!
SNAP!

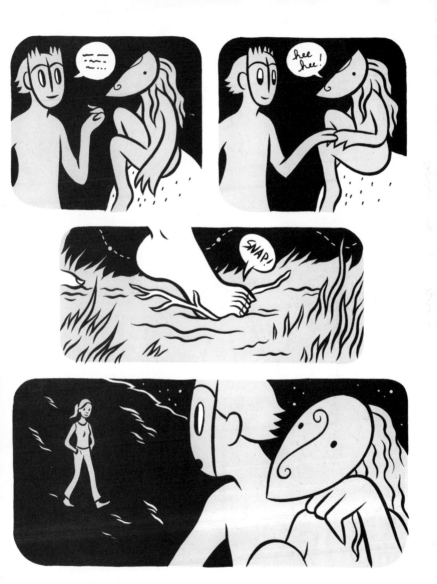

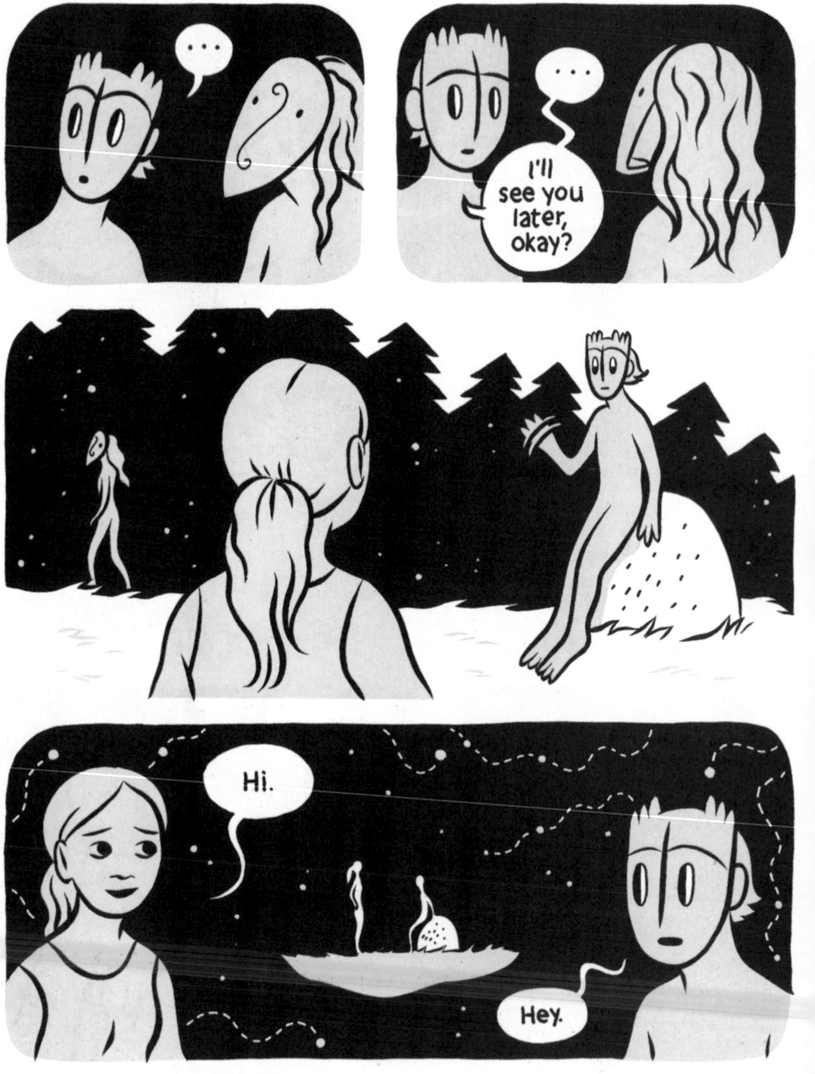
...
...
I'll see you later, okay?
Hi.
Hey.

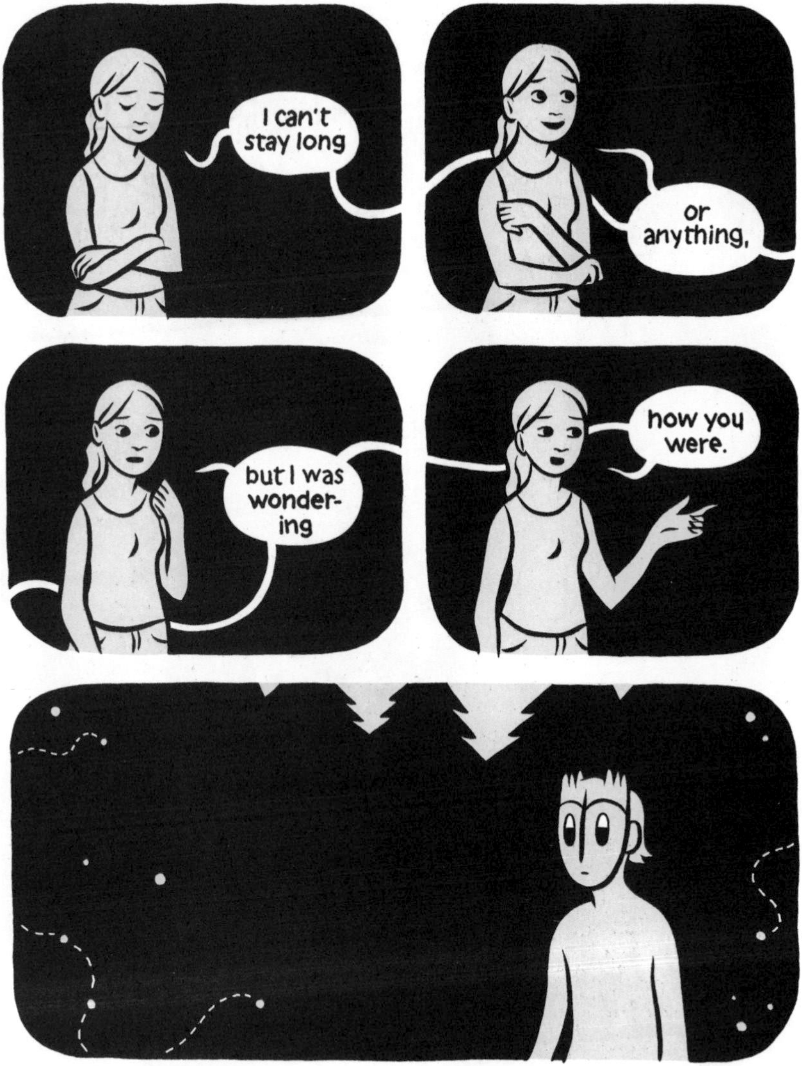
I can't stay long
or anything,
but I was wondering
how you were.

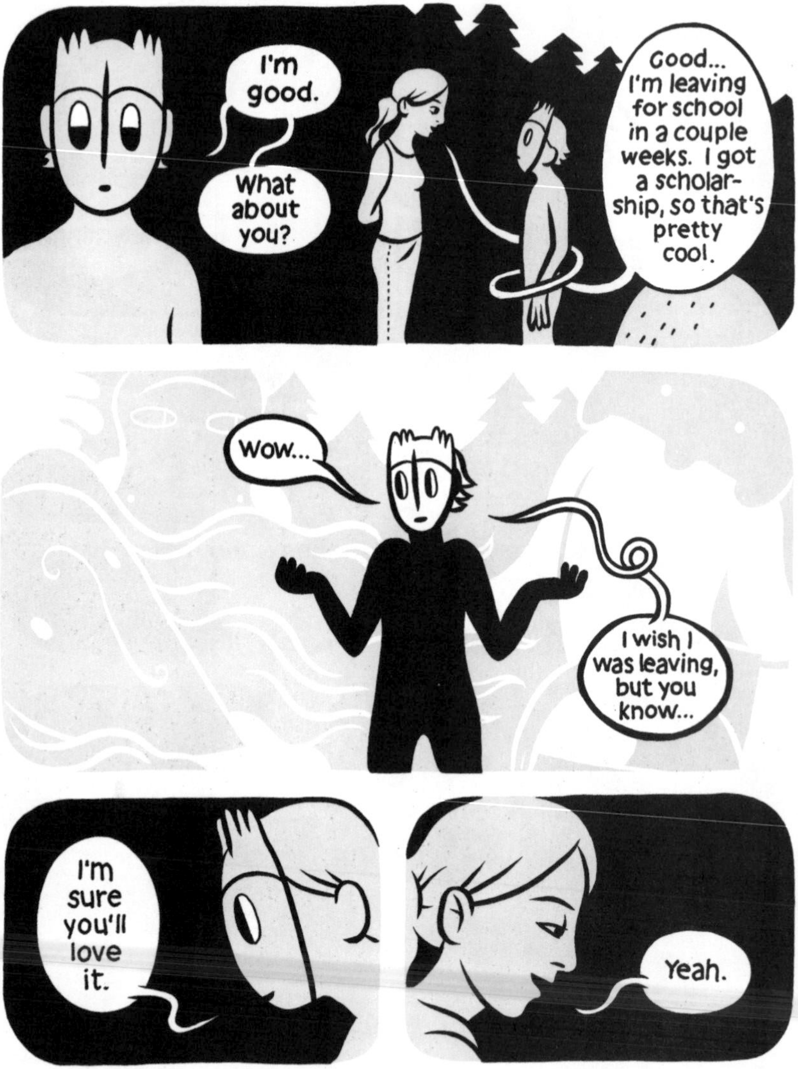
I'm good.
What about you?
Good... I'm leaving for school in a couple weeks. I got a scholar-ship, so that's pretty cool.
Wow...
I wish I was leaving, but you know...
I'm sure you'll love it.
Yeah.

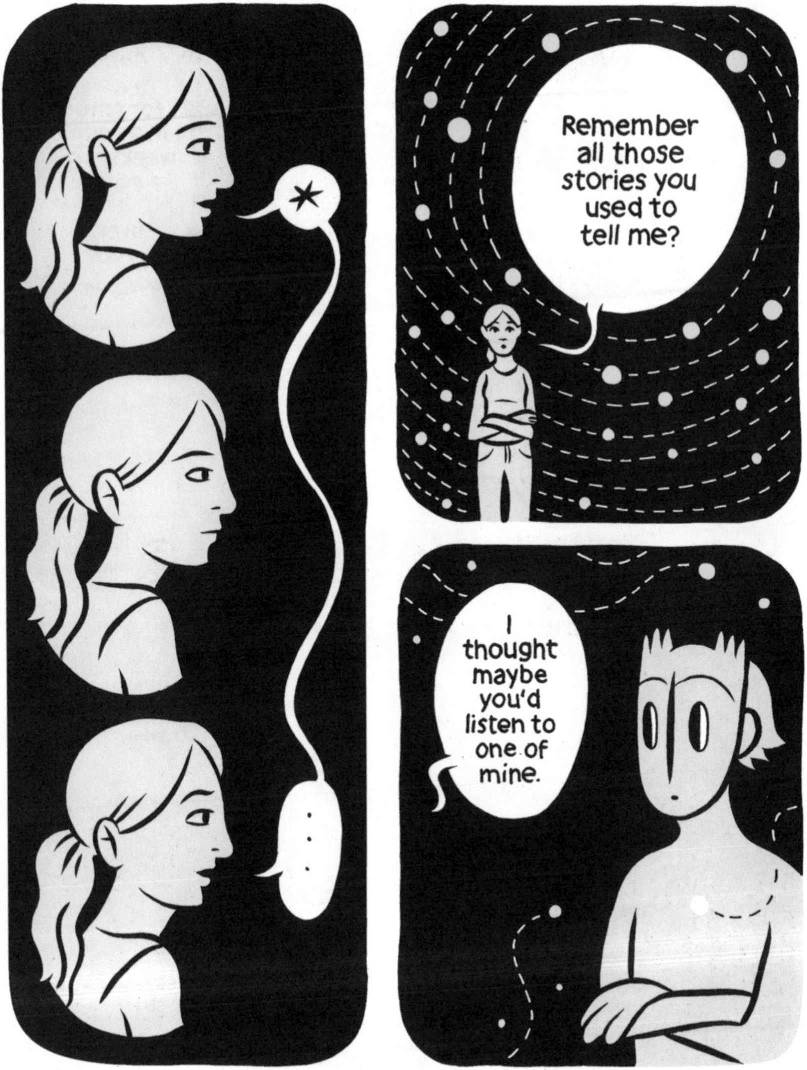
*
...
Remember all those stories you used to tell me?
I thought maybe you'd listen to one of mine.

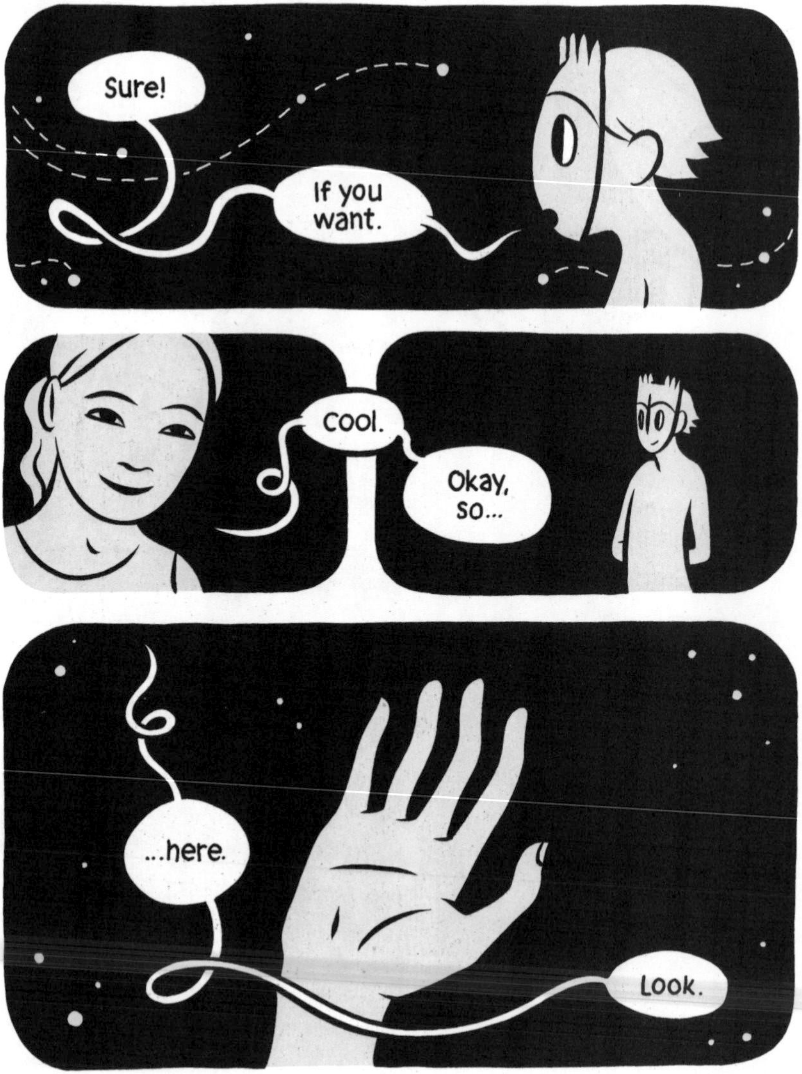
Sure!
If you want.
Cool.
Okay, so...
...here.
Look.

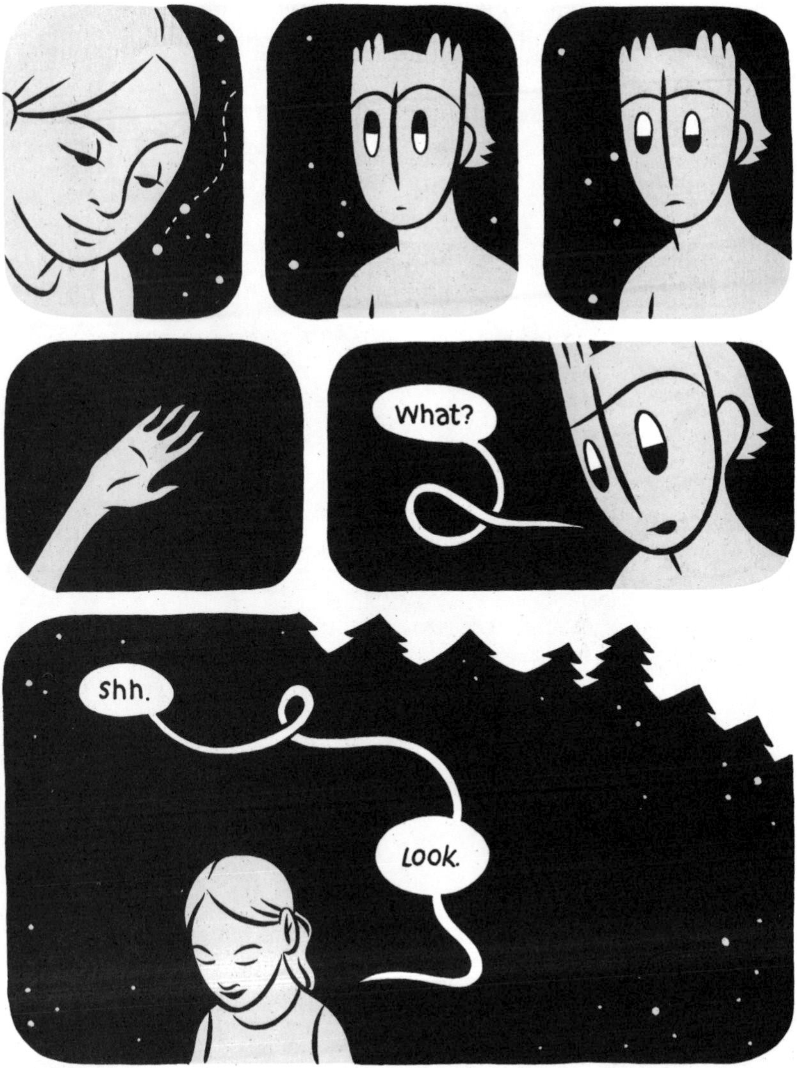
What?
Shh.
Look.

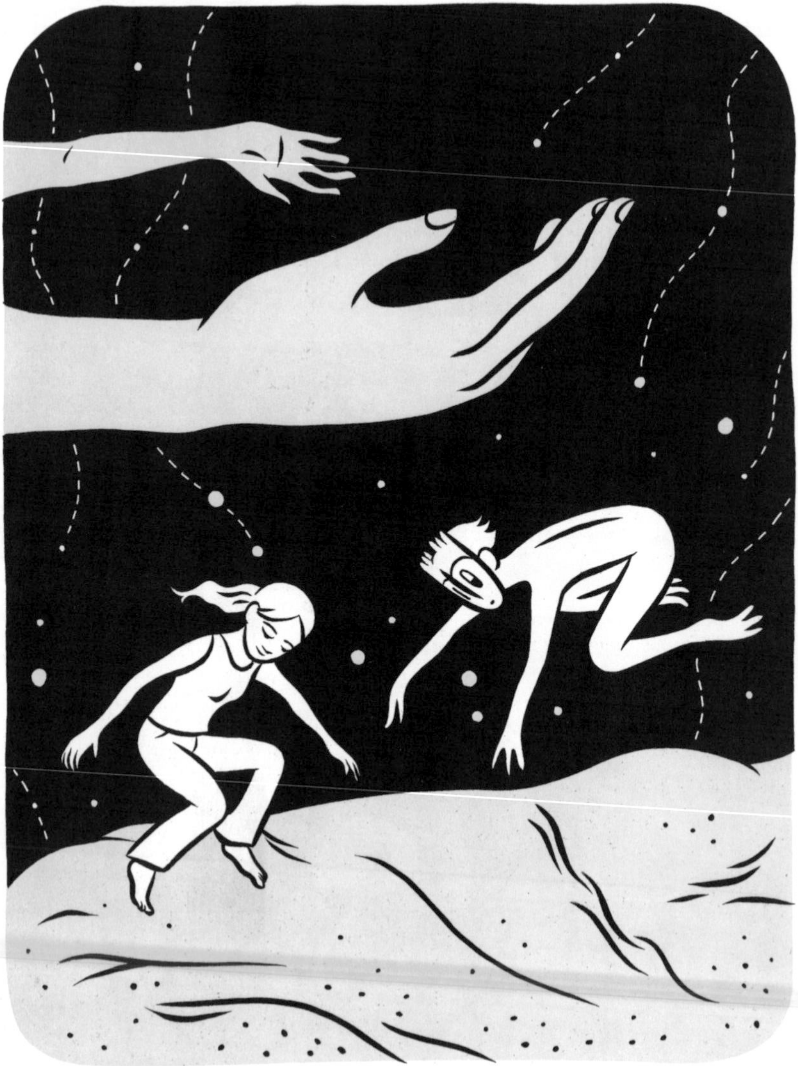

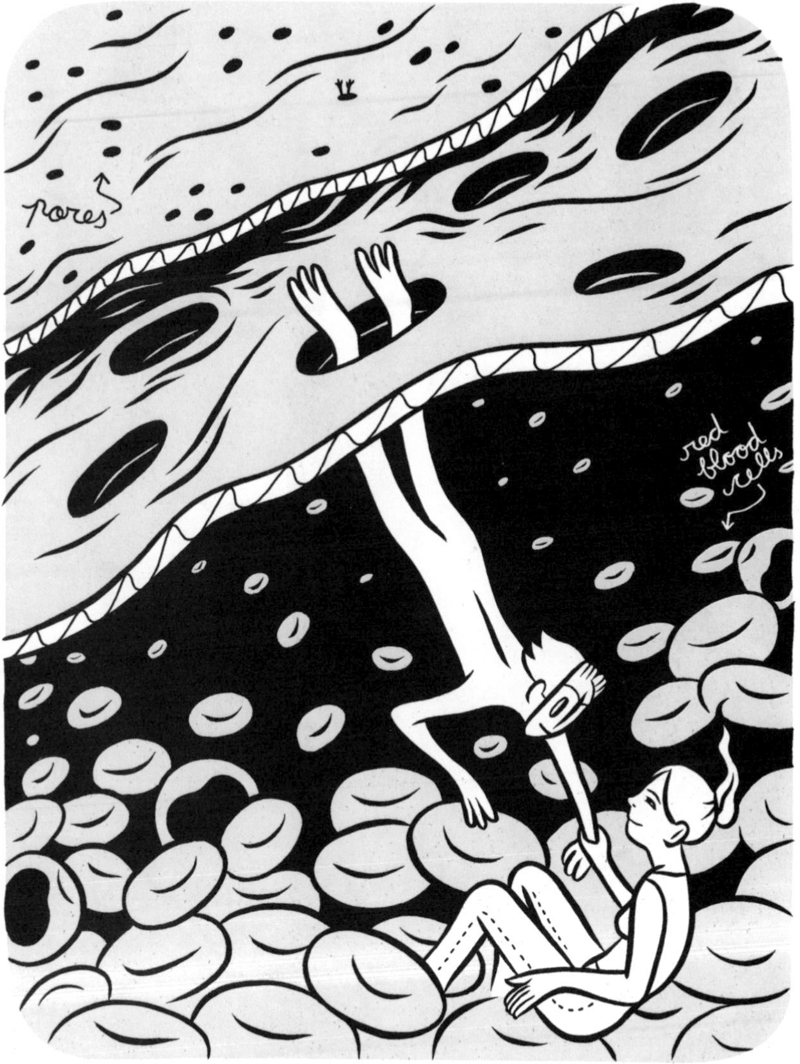
pores
red blood cells

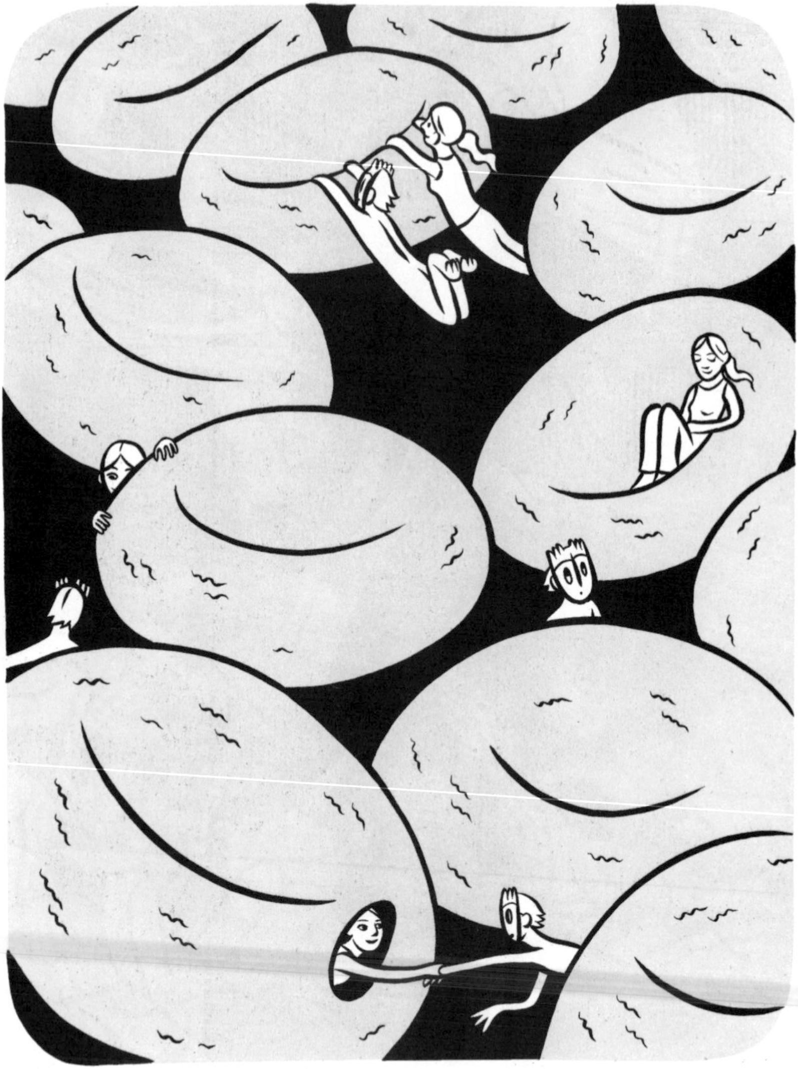

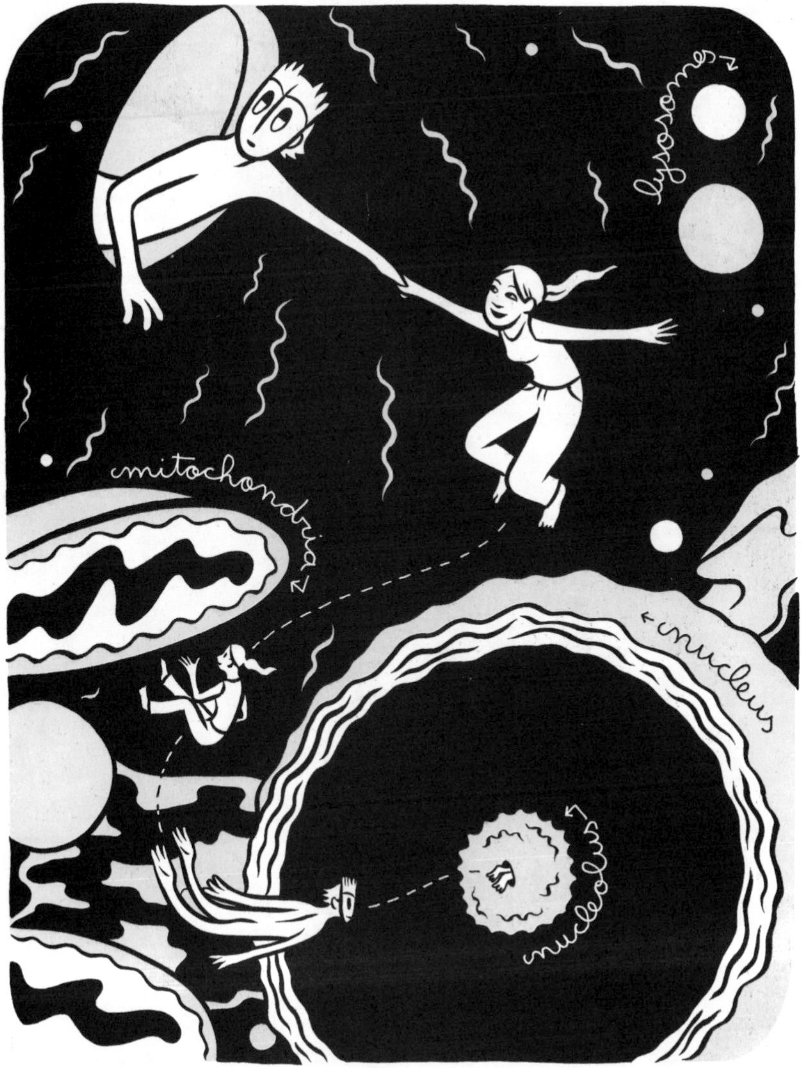
lysosomes
mitochondria
nucleus
nucleolus

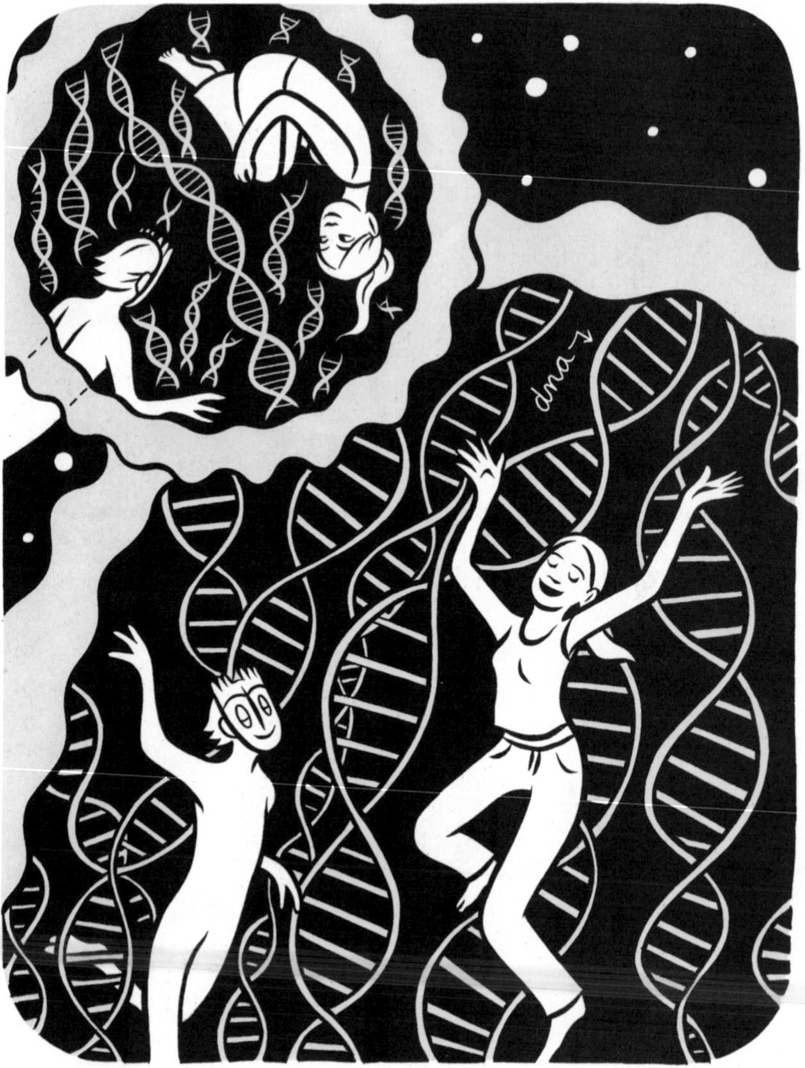
dna

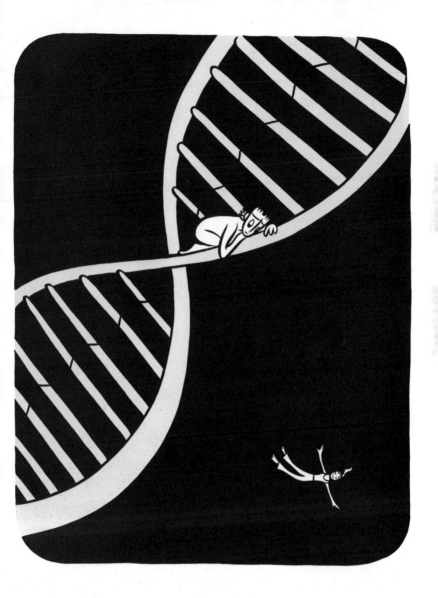

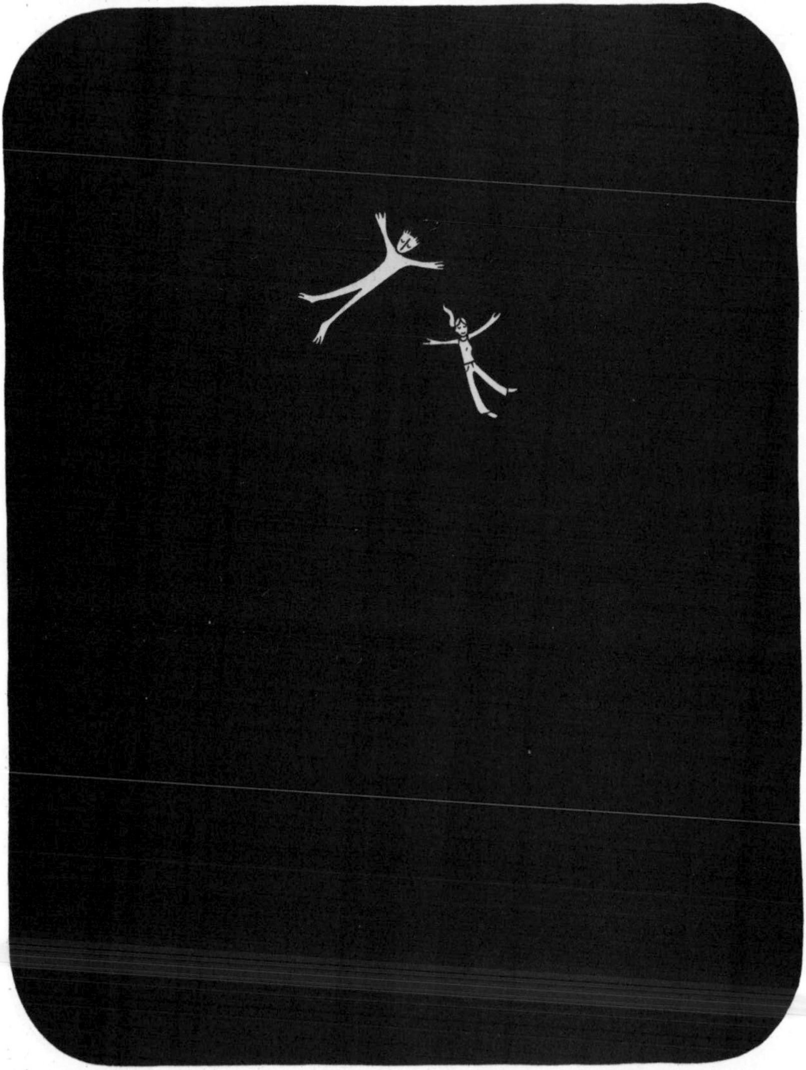

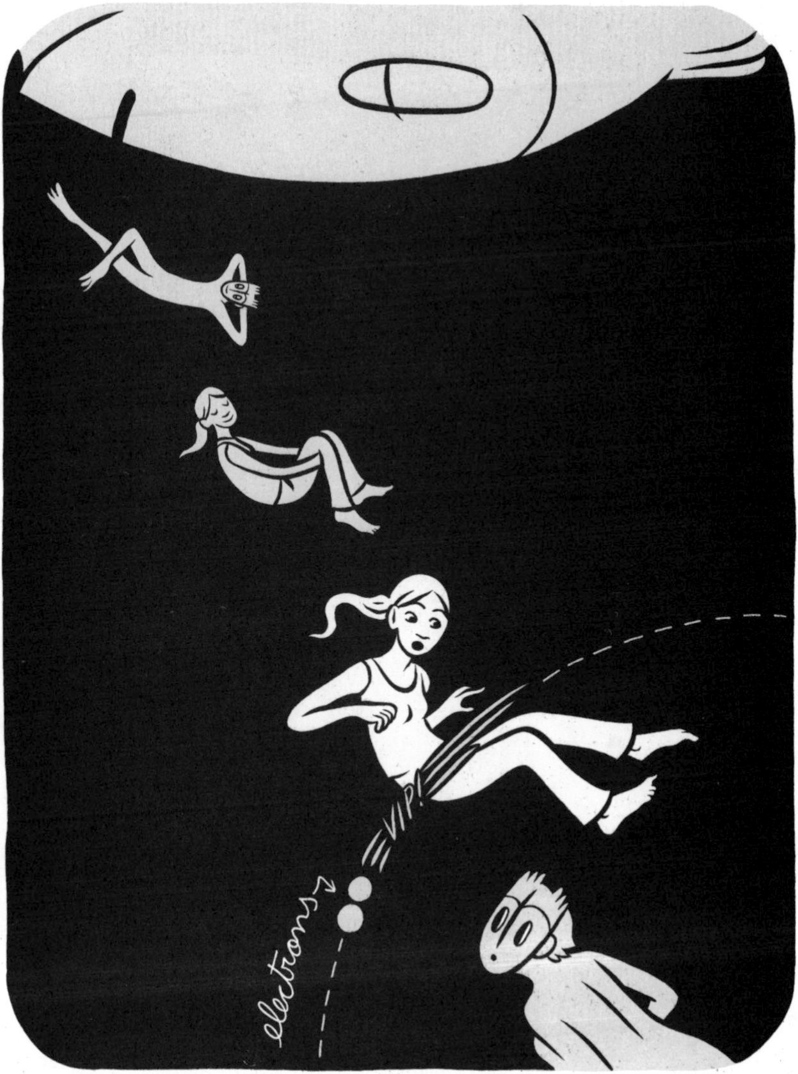
VIP!
electrons

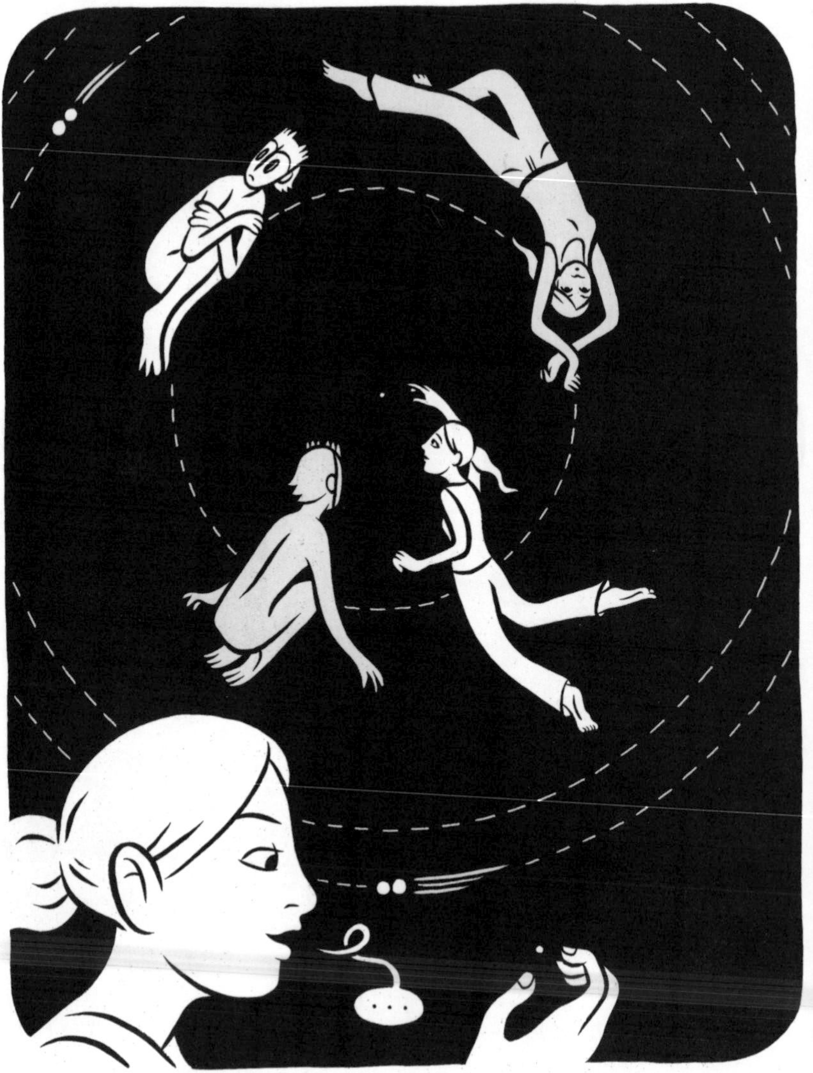

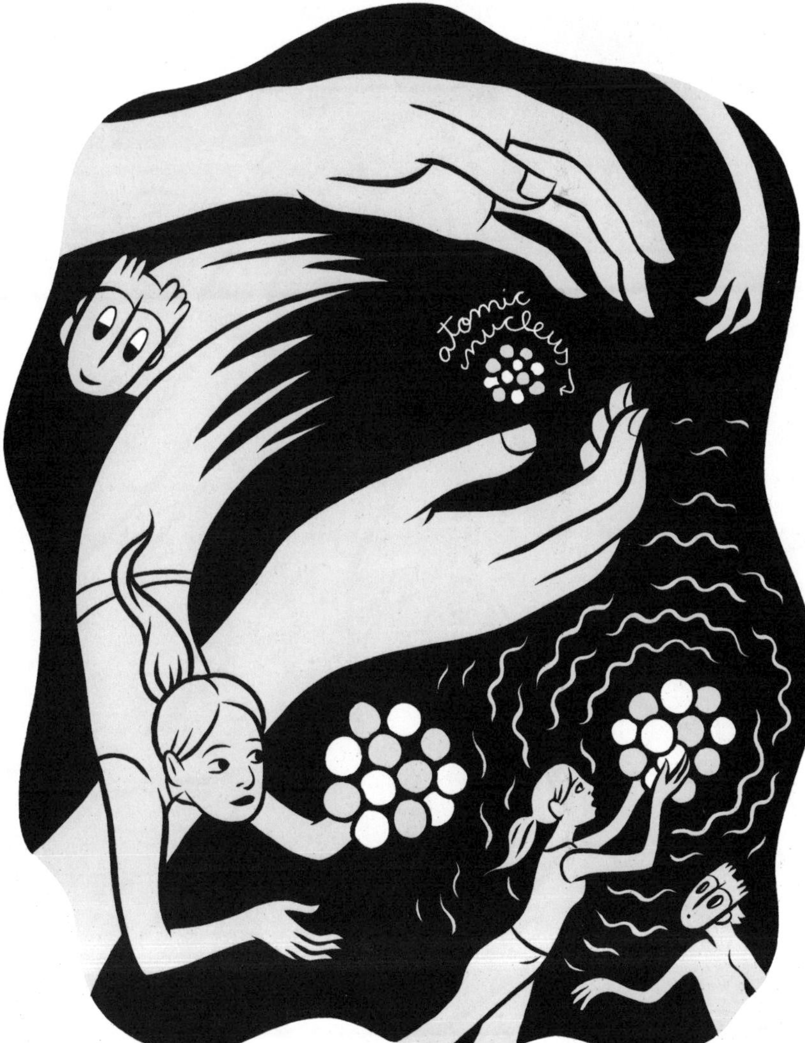
atomic nucleus

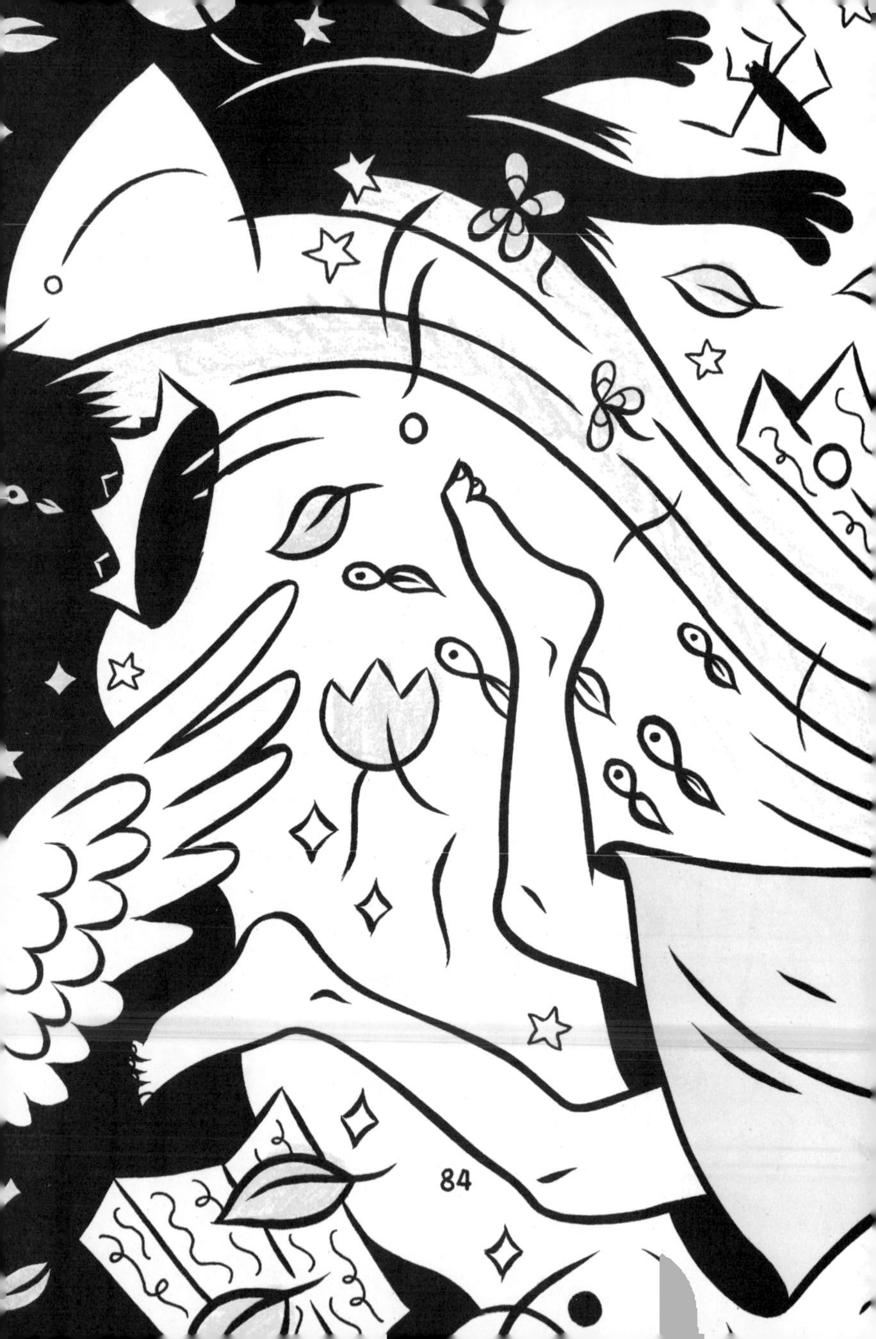

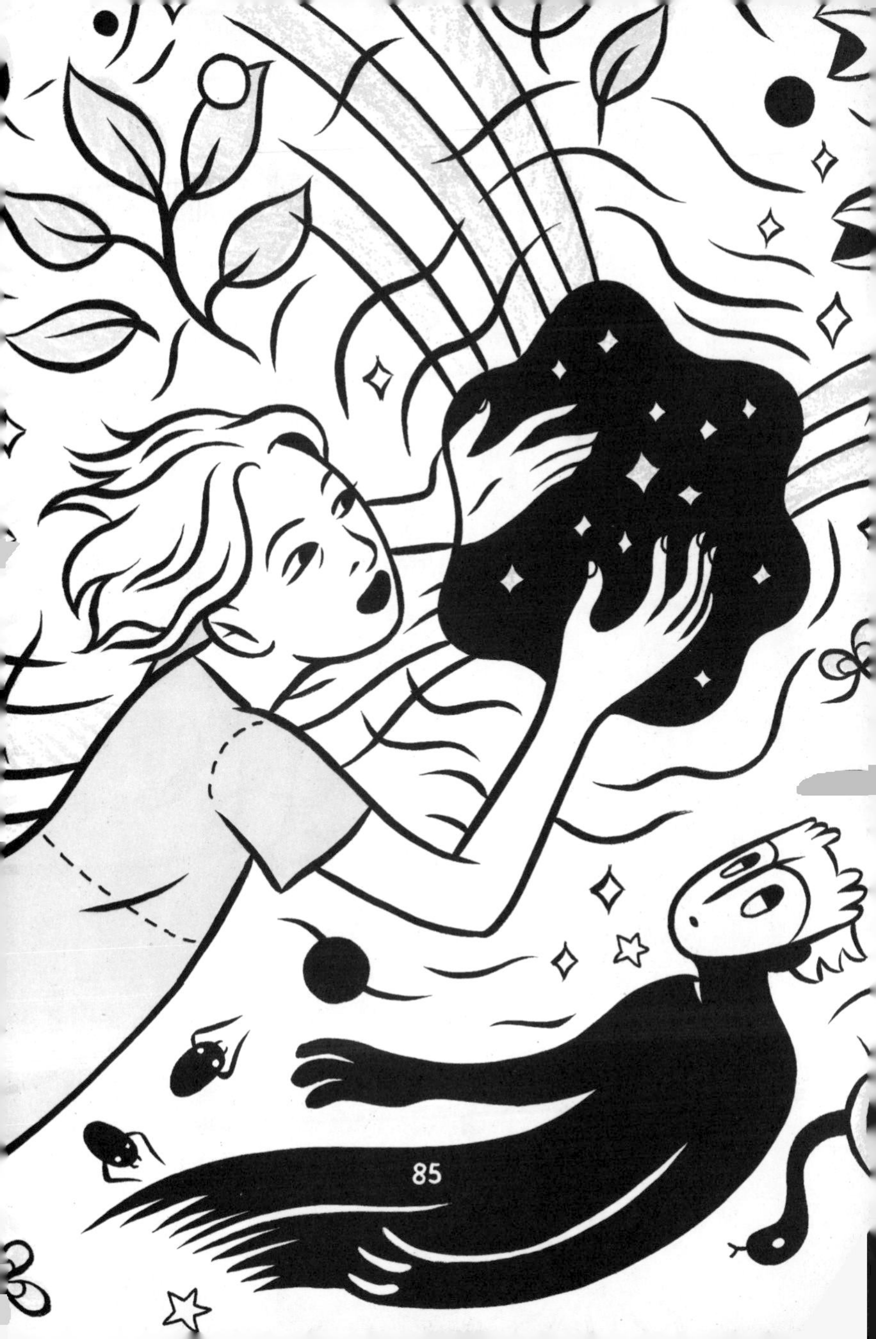

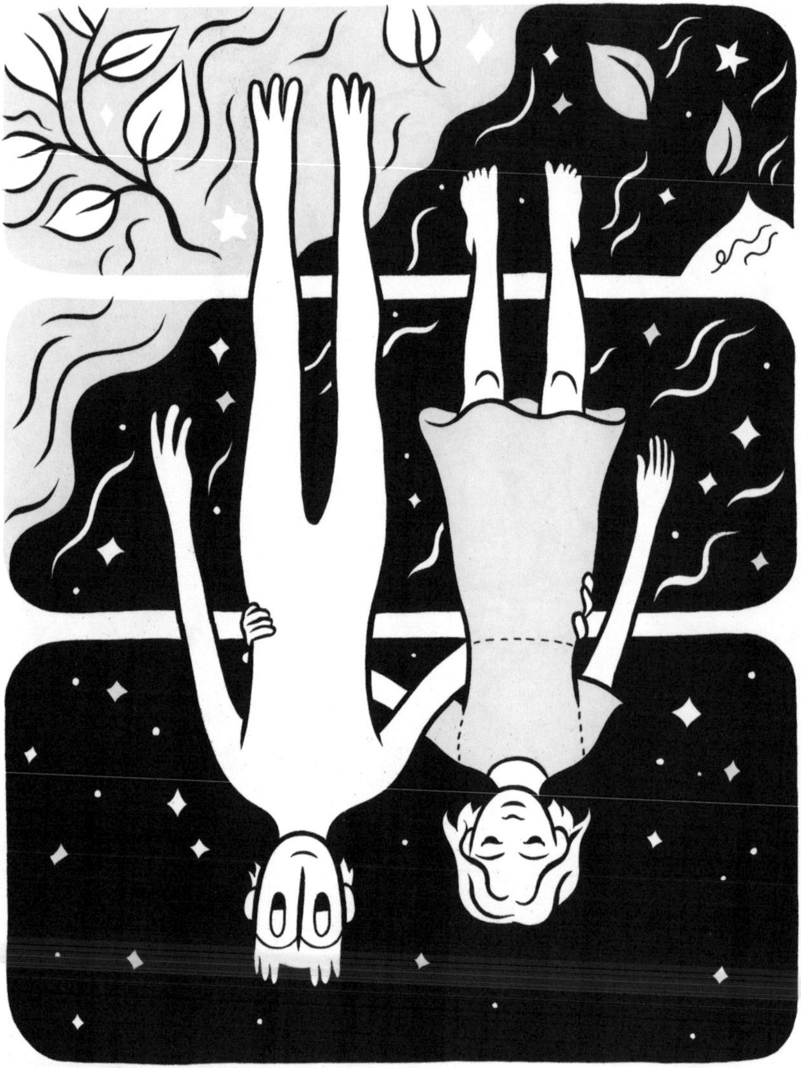

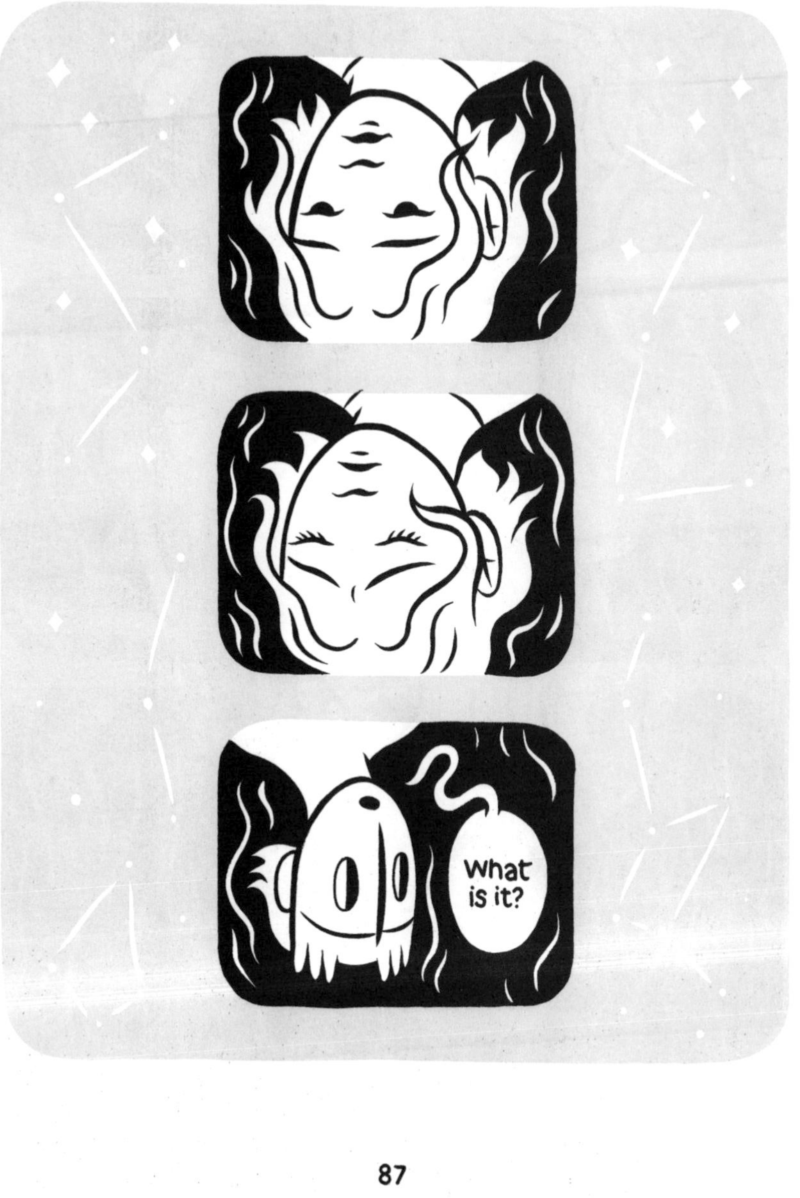
What is it?

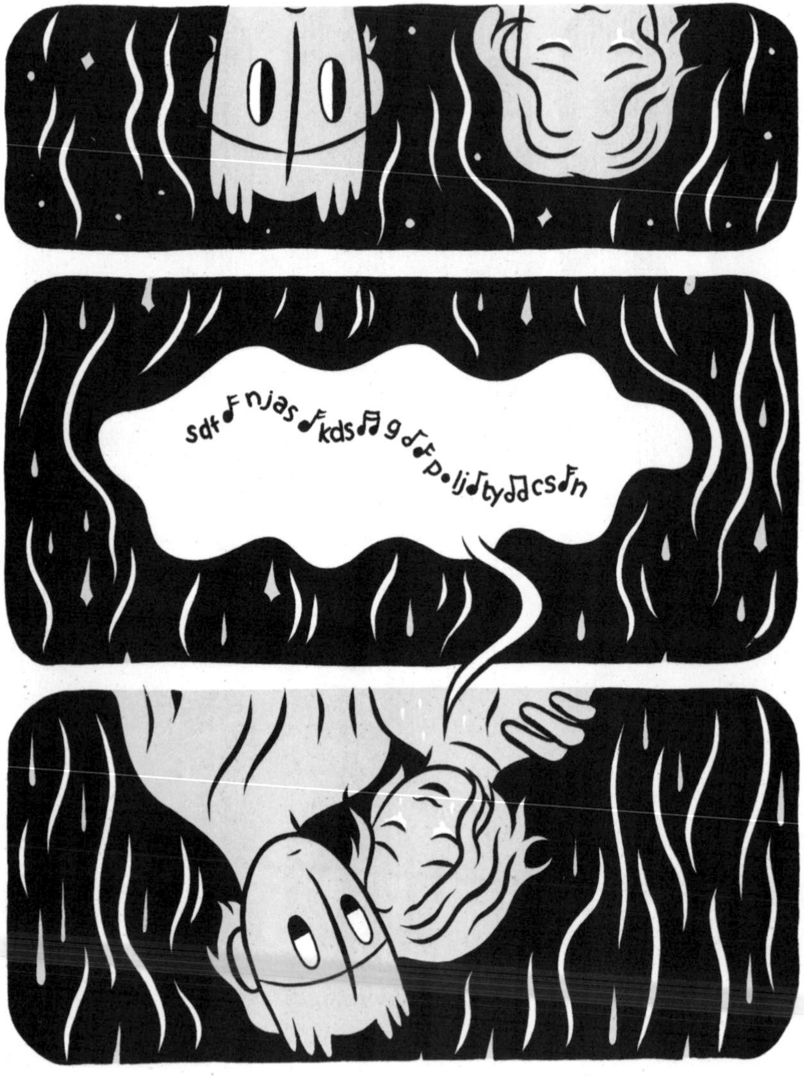
sdf♪njas♪kds♫g♪♪p•lj♪ty♫cs♪n

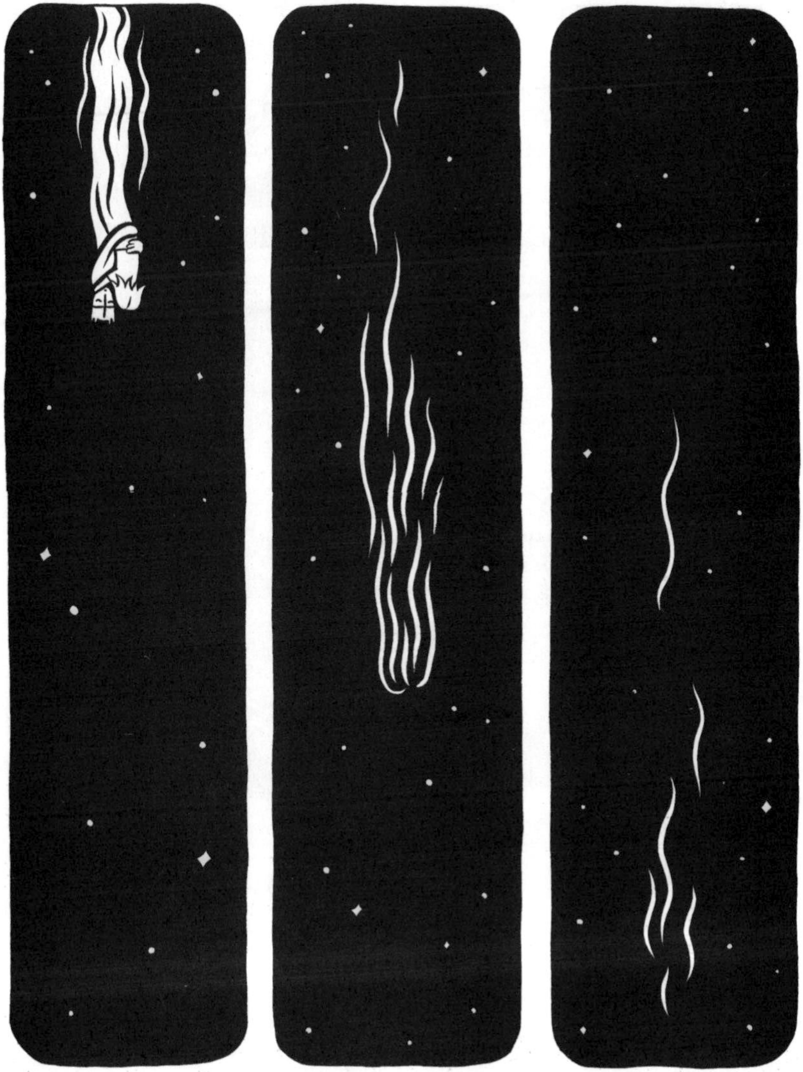

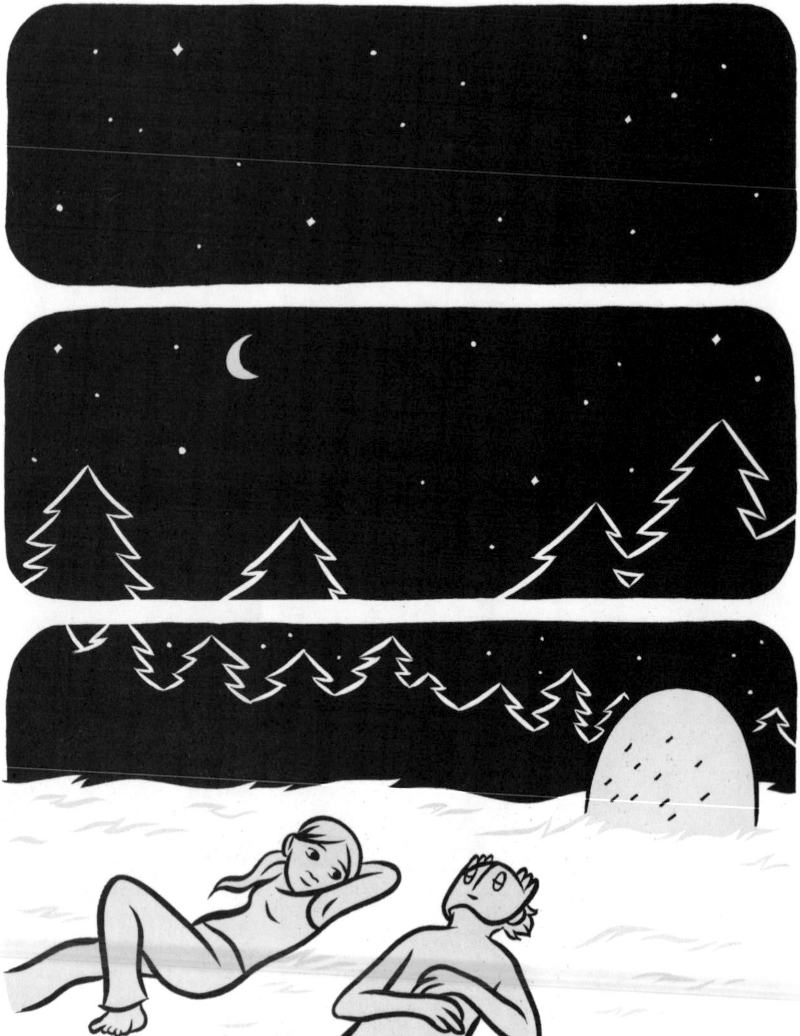

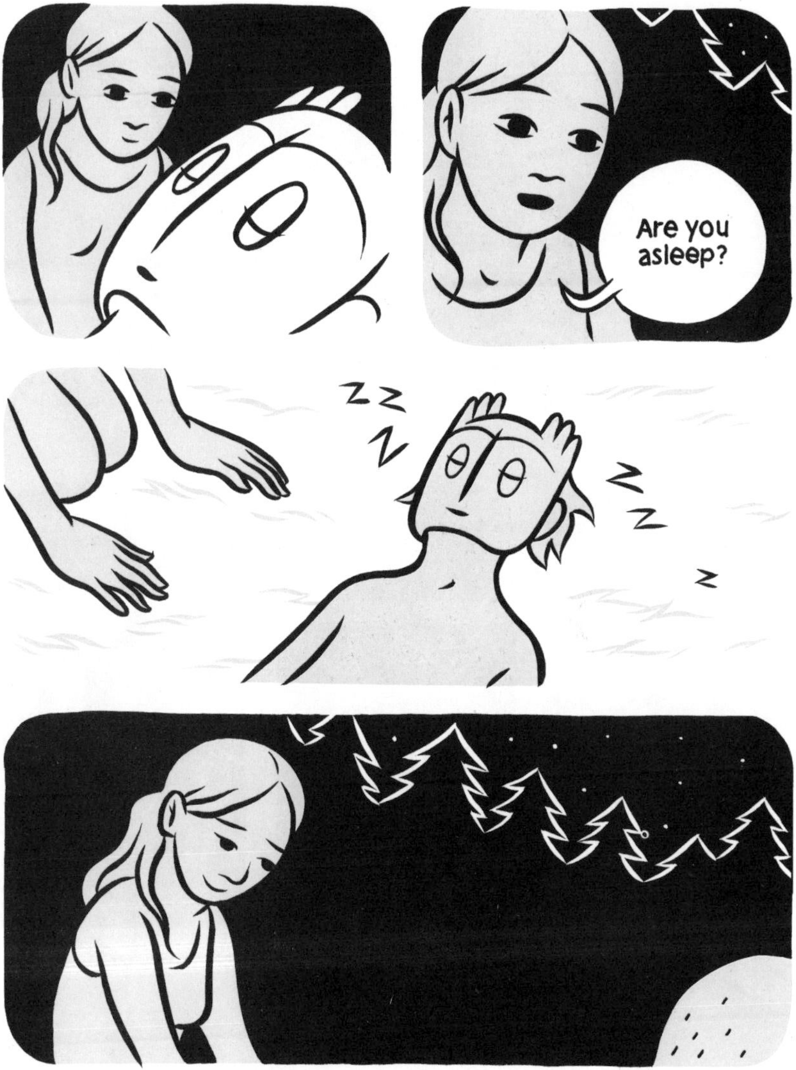
Are you asleep?
ZZ
Z
Z
Z
Z

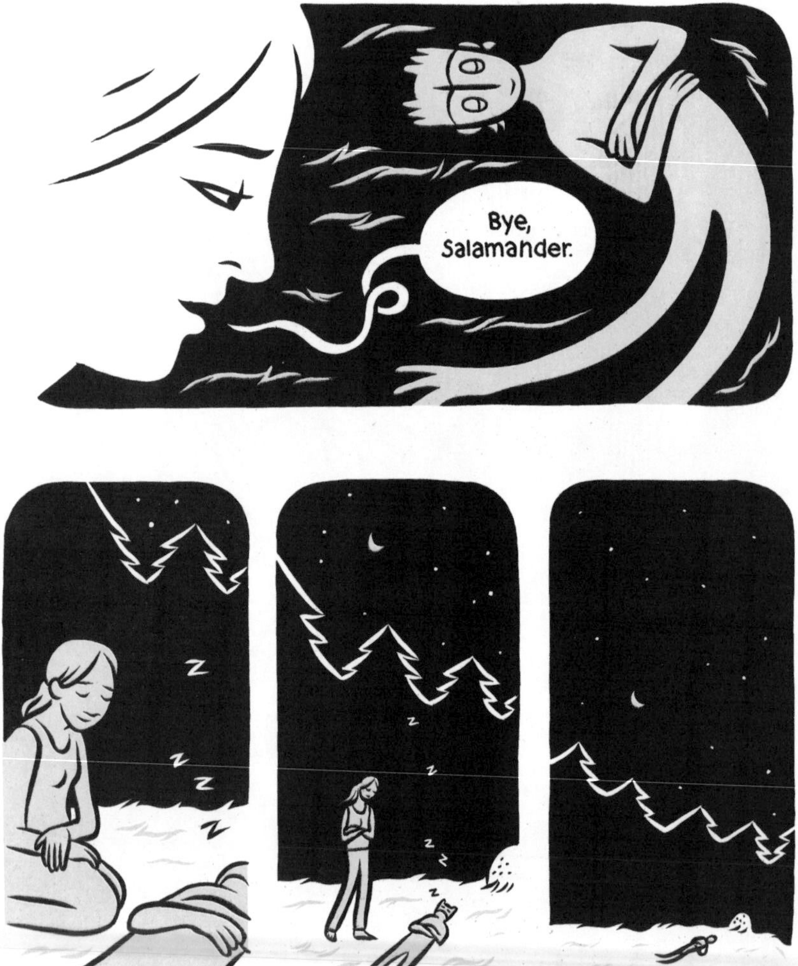
Bye, Salamander.

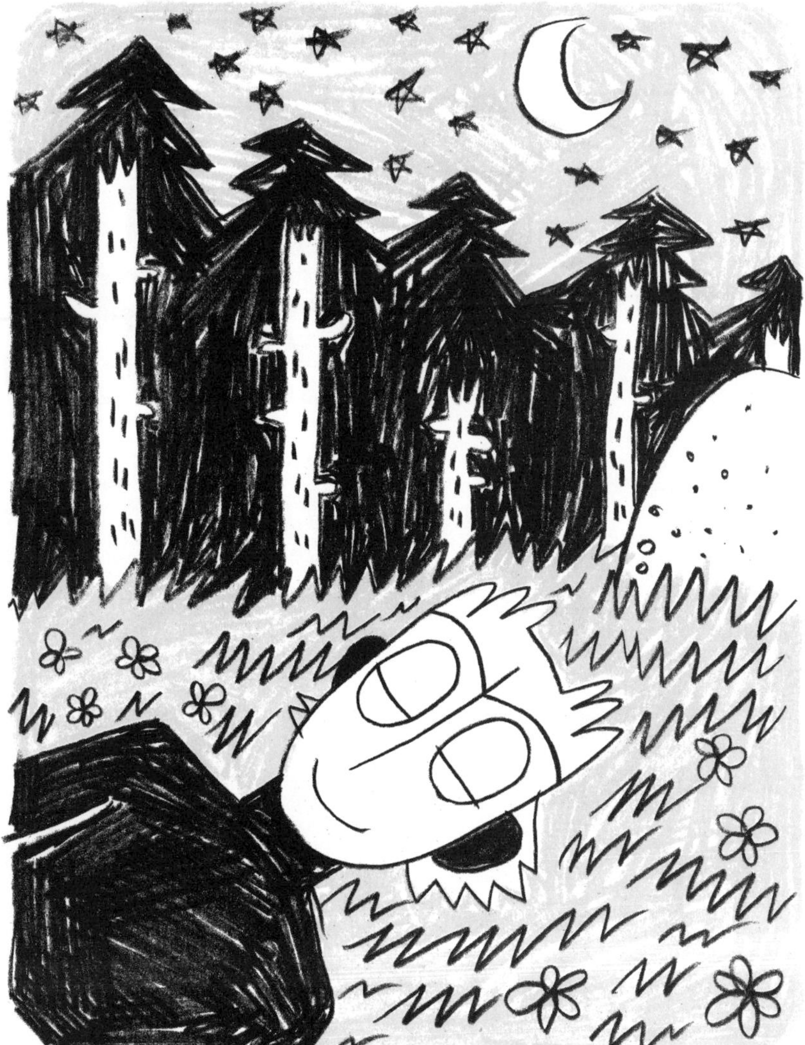

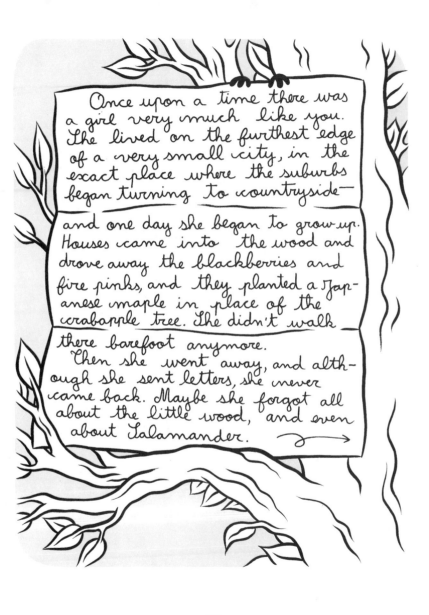

Once upon a time there was a girl very much like you. She lived on the furthest edge of a very small city, in the exact place where the suburbs began turning to countryside—

and one day she began to grow up. Houses came into the wood and drove away the blackberries and fire pinks, and they planted a Japanese maple in place of the crabapple tree. She didn't walk there barefoot anymore.

Then she went away, and although she sent letters, she never came back. Maybe she forgot all about the little wood, and even about Salamander. ⟶

but maybe she found
another place in the world

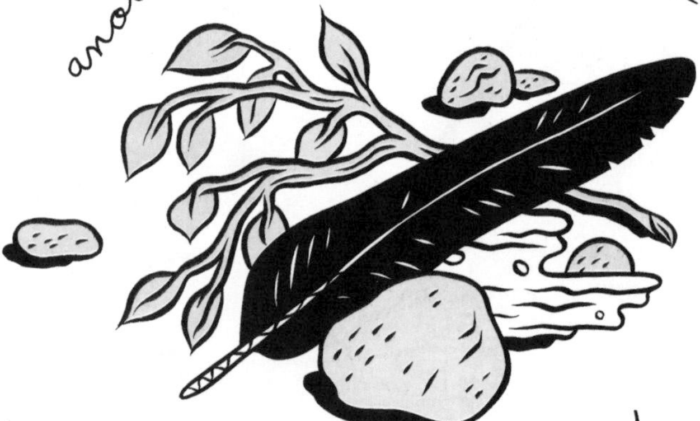

with a wood, and a field
with a creek running
through it,

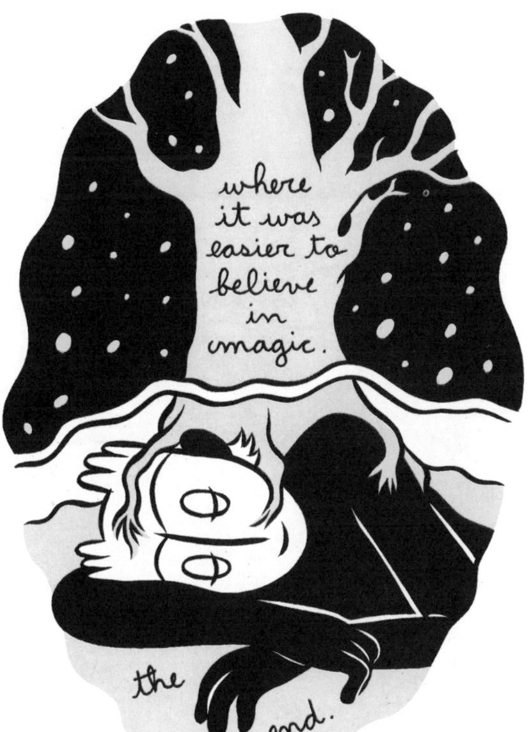
where
it was
easier to
believe
in
magic.
the
end.

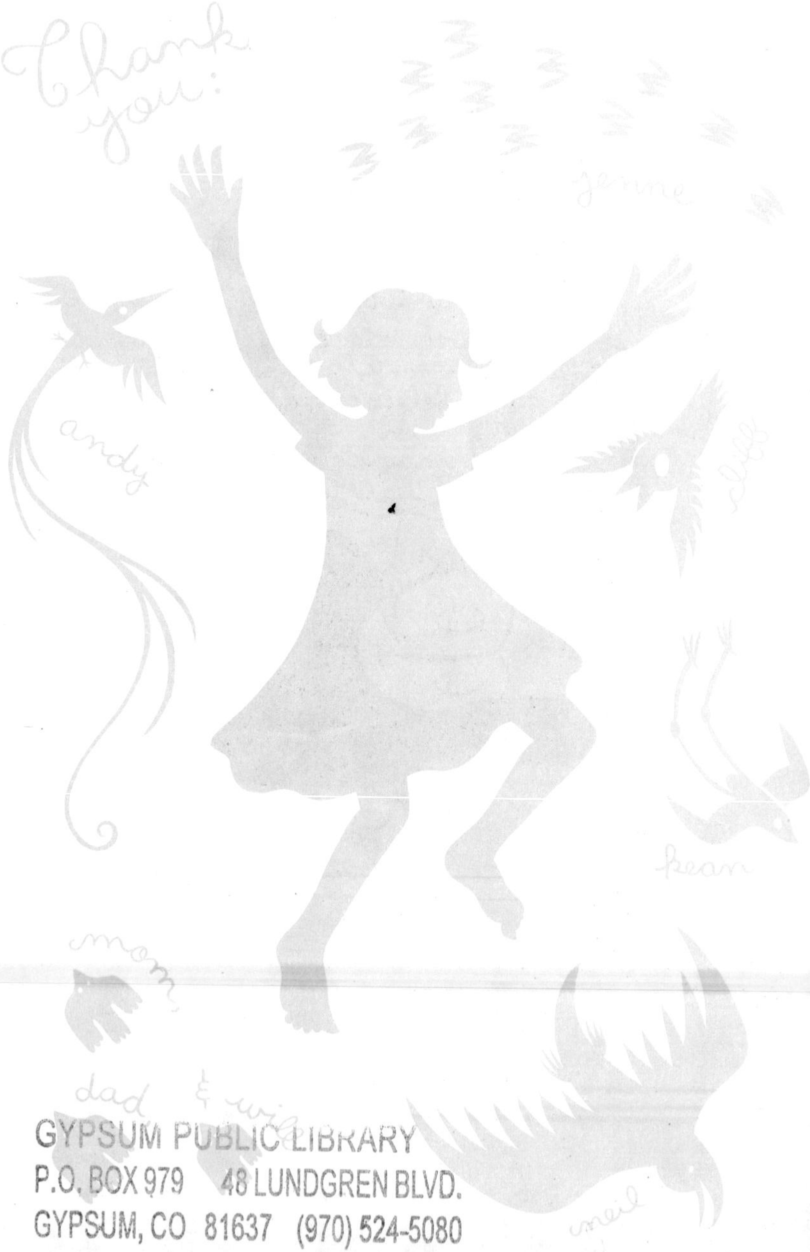
Thank you:
jenne
andy
cliff
bean
mom
dad & wi
neil